TABLE OF CONTENTS

The student pages in this book have been specially prepared for reproduction on any standard copying machine.

Permission is hereby granted to the purchaser of this book to reproduce student pages for classroom use only. Reproduction for commercial resale or for an entire school or school system is strictly prohibited. No part of this book may be reproduced for storage in a retrieval system, or transmitted in any form, by any means (electronic, recording, mechanical,or otherwise) without the prior written permission of the publisher.

Kelley Wingate products are available at fine educational supply stores throughout the U.S. and Canada.

Writing Grade 4   CD-3719   Printed in the United States of America   ISBN 0-88724-437-8

A NOTE TO PARENTS AND TEACHERS

Children are natural storytellers. Most of them can hardly wait to recount their experiences to their teacher or friends. An important task of the parent and teacher is to turn these storytellers into story writers. Children who begin to write early become comfortable with the process. Writing becomes as natural as speaking. It is important to make writing a part of the daily schedule.

Many children find writing difficult because they do not understand how to write. They do not even know how to begin. Any writing activity must be modeled by the teacher several times before a child can grasp the concepts. To achieve the greatest affect, the activity should be conducted with a group. This allows the free exchange of ideas and prompts deeper thinking that will assist in better clarity and comprehension of the concepts. When the task is fully understood and mastered within groups, individual assignments become appropriate.

Writing is a process, and it takes time to develop ideas into a finished product. Neither the teacher nor student should expect a well designed story to emerge from an initial attempt. Teachers and students should look upon writing as a five step process. The first step is gathering ideas pertaining to the writing assignment. The second step is selecting and organizing those ideas into a rough draft. Third is the revising step to reorganize content and refine wording. The fourth step is editing (proofreading) for grammar, capitalization, and punctuation errors. Lastly, the paper is rewritten as a final copy. Remember to use these five steps to guide the writing process.

Students do willingly what they do well. Direct instruction, ample opportunities to practice skills, and exciting topics will support these storytellers in our quest to make them story writers.

About the author...

During her many years as an educator, **Rae Anne Roberson** has taught in elementary, junior and senior high, and university level settings. She is currently the Title 1 Instructional Facilitator in her school system and is helping to develop several innovative reading programs for "at risk" students in elementary schools. Rae Anne is very active as a presenter at workshops for teachers and parents. She was recently presented with the "Award for Literacy" for her school system. Certified in elementary and secondary education as well as reading specialist, Rae Anne holds an M.Ed. and is currently working toward her doctorate.

Senior Editors: Patricia Pedigo and Roger DeSanti
Production Supervisor: Homer Desrochers
Production: Arlene Evitts and Debra Ollier

Ready-To-Use Ideas and Activities

The activities in this book will help students master the basic skills necessary to become competent writers. Remember as you read through the activities listed below, and as you go through this book, that all children learn at their own rate. Although repetition is important, it is critical that we never lose sight of the fact that it is equally important to build children's self-esteem and self-confidence if we want them to become successful learners as well as good citizens.

If you are working with a child at home, try to set up a quiet comfortable environment where you will work. Make it a special time to which you each look forward. Do only a few activities at a time. Try to end each session on a positive note, and remember that fostering self-esteem and self-confidence are also critical to the learning process.

The back of this book has removable flash cards that will be great for use for basic skill and vocabulary enrichment activities. Pull the flash cards out and either cut them apart or, if you have access to a paper cutter, use that to cut the flash cards apart.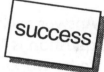

Following are checklists that students should use to help keep their sentence and paragraph writing on track.

Sentence Editing Checklist

Answer each question on this checklist either Yes or No. If your answer to any question is "No" or "I'm not sure," list that part of the report as a part that needs to be worked on.

Do most of your sentences say "who did what" and in that order?
❏ Yes ❏ No

Is every sentence complete?
❏ Yes ❏ No

Ready-To-Use Ideas and Activities

Does every sentence begin with a capital letter and end with a period, question mark, or exclamation point?
❏ Yes ❏ No

Are all your verbs in the same tense, either present or past?
❏ Yes ❏ No

Are all your sentences in the third person (unless your assignment says that you can use first or second person)?
❏ Yes ❏ No

Paragraph Editing Checklist

Answer each question on this checklist either Yes or No. If your answer to any question is "No" or "I'm not sure," list that part of your paper as a part that needs to be worked on.

Does each paragraph have a topic sentence?
❏ Yes ❏ No

Are your supporting details convincing?
❏ Yes ❏ No

Are the supporting details in logical order?
❏ Yes ❏ No

Have you tried to add special details or lively quotes?
❏ Yes ❏ No

Did you take out all dull or unnecessary information?
❏ Yes ❏ No

Have you removed sentences that don't belong with the others?
❏ Yes ❏ No

Ready-To-Use Ideas and Activities

Basic Outline Format
 Title

   I.   Opening
   II.   First Main Point or Idea
         A.   Supporting detail
         B.   More supporting detail
   III. Next Main Point or Idea
         A.   Supporting detail
         B.   More supporting detail
         C.   More supporting detail
   IV.   Last Main Point or Idea
         A.   Supporting detail
         B.   More supporting detail
         C.   More supporting detail
   V.   Conclusion

Reasons For Writing

Expose your students to the many types of writing that are out in the world. Newspapers, magazines, advertisements, weather forecasts, recipes, poems, automotive manuals, short stories, novels, personal letters, and more. Once students are exposed to the many forms of writing, chances are very good that interests will peak and writing will become more enjoyable.

Creative Writing
Ask students to read an article in the newspaper. Once read, have students rewrite the article with a different ending. This exercise is extremely effective in helping students understand the importance of supporting details. Other great creative writing activities include:
• Writing letters to the school principal
• Responding to an editorial in the newspaper
• Interviewing a family member
• Writing directions for assembling a kite

• Writing a recipe for a favorite food
• Writing a T.V. script
Correction Symbols

∧	add a word	◯	close the space
⌃	add a comma	≠	make a space
⊙	add a period	≡	capitalize
⌄	add an apostrophe	/	make lower case
⌄ ⌄	add quotation marks	SP	spelling error
ℯ	remove	¶	begin a new paragraph

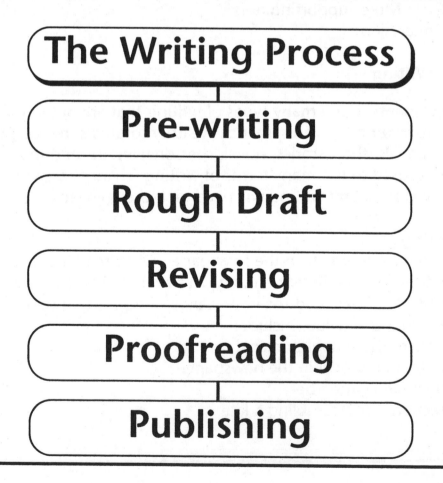

The Writing Process

Pre-writing

Rough Draft

Revising

Proofreading

Publishing

An invitation includes all the important facts.

"You are invited!" You must know <u>why</u>, <u>who</u>, <u>when</u>, and <u>where</u>. An invitation gives you all this information.

1. Read the invitation and answer the questions.

A CHRISTMAS PARTY!

Given by:	Randy Johns
Time:	7:00 p.m.
Date:	December 15
Place:	606 Lime Ave.

<u>Why</u> has the invitation been sent?

_____

<u>Who</u> is giving the party?

_____

<u>When</u> will you go?

_____

<u>Where</u> will you go?

_____

---

2. Write an invitation to a Going Away Party. List the important information and Write the information on the invitation.

<u>Why</u> will the invitation be sent?

_____

<u>Who</u> is giving the party?

_____

<u>When</u> is the party?

_____

<u>Where</u> is the party?

_____

Come Say Goodbye

Given by:	_____
Time:	_____
Date:	_____
Place:	_____

An invitation includes all the important facts.

"You are invited!" You must know <u>why</u>, <u>who</u>, <u>when</u>, and <u>where</u>. An invitation gives you all this information.

1. Read the invitation and answer the questions.

**Grand Opening:
Jerry's Jeans Shop**

Given by:	Jerry Adams
Time:	10:00 a.m.
Date:	August 17
Place:	Lakeland Mall

<u>Why</u> has the invitation been sent?

_____

<u>Who</u> is giving the party?

_____

<u>When</u> will you go?

_____

<u>Where</u> will you go?

_____

2. Write an invitation to the opening of "Different Spokes for Different Folks Bike Store". List the important information. Write the information on the invitation.

<u>Why</u> will the invitation be sent?

_____

<u>Who</u> is giving the party?

_____

<u>When</u> is the party?

_____

<u>Where</u> is the party?

_____

Wheel On In!

Given by: _____

Time: _____

Date: _____

Place: _____

An invitation includes all the important facts.

"You are invited!" You must know <u>why</u>, <u>who</u>, <u>when</u>, and <u>where</u>. An invitation gives you all this information.

---

1. Read the invitation and answer the questions.

Come One, Come All!   **Taft Park School**   **Talent Show**
Given by: 4th Grade
Time: 7:00 p.m.
Date: October 20
Place: Taft Park Elementary   School

<u>Why</u> has the invitation been sent?

_____

<u>Who</u> is giving the talent show?

_____

<u>When</u> will you go?

_____

<u>Where</u> will you go?

_____

---

2. Write an invitation for a school open house. List the important information. Write the information on the invitation.

<u>Why</u> will the invitation be sent?

_____

<u>Who</u> is giving the open house?

_____

<u>When</u> is the open house?

_____

<u>Where</u> is the open house?

_____

OPEN HOUSE   **PLEASE COME!**
Given by:_____
Time: _____
Date: _____
Place: _____

An invitation includes all the important facts.

"You are invited!" You must know <u>why</u>, <u>who</u>, <u>when</u>, and <u>where</u>. An invitation gives you all this information.

1. Read the invitation answer the questions.

RAE'S BOWL-A-RAMA
After School Special - Half Price Games

Given by: Rae Lowe

Time: 3:00 -5:00 p.m.

Date: Monday - Friday

Place: Rae's Bowl-a-Rama
                  Jefferson Avenue

<u>Why</u> has the invitation been sent?

_____

<u>Who</u> is giving the party?

_____

<u>When</u> will you go?

_____

<u>Where</u> will you go?

_____

2. Write an invitation to a swimming party. List the important information. Write the information on the invitation.

<u>Why</u> will the invitation be sent?

_____

<u>Who</u> is giving the party?

_____

<u>When</u> is the party?

_____

<u>Where</u> is the party?

_____

YOU ARE INVITED!

Given by: _____

Time: _____

Date: _____

Place: _____

| An invitation includes all the important facts. |

"You are invited!" You must know <u>why</u>, <u>who</u>, <u>when</u>, and <u>where</u>. An invitation gives you all this information.

1. Read the invitation and answer the questions

IT'S OUR ANNIVERSARY!

Given by:	Norman and Grace Davis
Time:	8:00 p.m.
Date:	July 12
Place:	41 Ashley Drive

<u>Why</u> has the invitation been sent?

_____

<u>Who</u> is giving the party?

_____

<u>When</u> will you go?

_____

<u>Where</u> will you go?

_____

2. Write an invitation to a barbeque. List the important information. Write the information on the invitation.

<u>Why</u> will the invitation be sent?

_____

<u>Who</u> is giving the barbeque?

_____

<u>When</u> is the barbeque?

_____

<u>Where</u> is the barbeque?

_____

COME JOIN US!

Given by:	_____
Time:	_____
Date:	_____
Place:	_____

An invitation includes all the important facts.

"You are invited!" You must know <u>why</u>, <u>who</u>, <u>when</u>, and <u>where</u>. An invitation gives you all this information.

1. Make your own invitation and answer the questions

Given by: _____

Time: _____

Date: _____

Place: _____

<u>Why</u> has the invitation been sent?

_____

<u>Who</u> is giving the party?

_____

<u>When</u> will you go?

_____

<u>Where</u> will you go?

_____

2. Make your own invitation. List the important information. Write the information on the invitation.

<u>Why</u> will the invitation be sent?

_____

<u>Who</u> is giving the party?

_____

<u>When</u> is the party?

_____

<u>Where</u> is the party?

_____

Given by: _____

Time: _____

Date: _____

Place: _____

It is important to address an envelope correctly. An envelope shows who is sending a letter and who is receiving a letter. Name, address, city, state, and zip code must be placed in the proper places.

The sender is : A
His house address is : B
His city, state, and zip code are : C

The receiver is : D
His house address is : E
His city, state, and zip code are : F

1. Study the completed envelope.

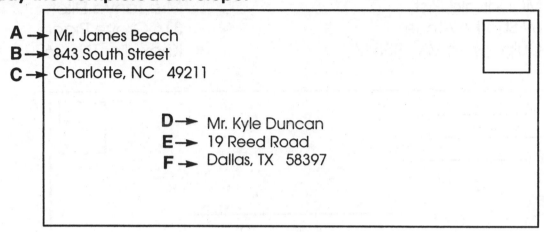

A → Mr. James Beach
B → 843 South Street
C → Charlotte, NC   49211

D → Mr. Kyle Duncan
E → 19 Reed Road
F → Dallas, TX   58397

2. Address the envelope below with the information given.

The sender is:
   Miss Kelly Tulver
   181 Crest Road
   Canton, MS   70125

The receiver is:
   Mrs. Dianne Baker
   89 Barron Street
   Albany, NY   25736

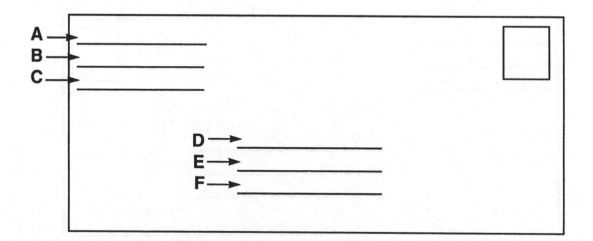

It is important to address an envelope correctly. An envelope shows who is sending a letter and who is receiving a letter. Name, address, city, state, and zip code must be placed in the proper places.

Address the envelopes below with the information given.

The sender is:
Mr. Donald First
69 Short Avenue
Culpepper, VA   88547

The receiver is:
Mrs. Tanya Elliot
316 Grove Place
Knoxville, TN   26791

The sender is:
Ms. Nancy Smith
74 Duncan Drive
Trenton, NJ   69275

The receiver is:
Miss Gail Russell
637 Lark Street
Portland, OR   57812

It is important to address an envelope correctly. An envelope shows who is sending a letter and who is receiving a letter. Name, address, city, state, and zip code must be placed in the proper places.

Address the envelopes below with the information given.

The sender is:
Dr. John Little
45 Meadow Place
Providence, RI 95672

The receiver is:
Ms. Janet Munch
75 Robin Blvd.
Denver, CO 74013

The sender is:
Mrs. Lucy Kline
909 Pine Ave.
Seattle, WA 44307

The receiver is:
Miss Pat Bullard
4405 York Street
Lansing, MI 56233

It is important to address an envelope correctly. An envelope shows who is sending a letter and who is receiving a letter. Name, address, city, state, and zip code must be placed in the proper places.

Address the envelopes below with the information given.

The sender is:
Dr. Mary Howard
344 Richland Avenue
Fargo, ND 77409

The receiver is:
Mr. Bob Alden
378 Sunset Blvd.
Tripp, SD 89345

The sender is:
Mr Harry Webster
40 Lincoln Lane
Tyrone, NM 34068

The receiver is:
Mrs. Kerry Rogers
670 Maine Street
Fairfield, KY 45569

It is important to address an envelope correctly. An envelope shows who is sending a letter and who is receiving a letter. Name, address, city, state, and zip code must be placed in the proper places.

Address the envelopes below with the information given.

The sender is:
Miss Rhonda Walter
660 Third Street
Chicago, IL 55098

The receiver is:
Mrs. Carla George
23 W. 42nd Street
Tampa, FL 21563

The sender is:
Mr. Fred Barrow
216 Dawson Drive
Ogden, UT 66065

The receiver is:
Ms. Jean Kesson
44123 Jasper Avenue
Concord, NH 55460

It is important to address an envelope correctly. An envelope shows who is sending a letter and who is receiving a letter. Name, address, city, state, and zip code must be placed in the proper places.

1. Address the envelope below to a friend.

2. Address the envelope below to a relative of yours.

| A friendly letter has 5 parts: date, greeting, body, closing, and signature. |

1. Read the following letter.

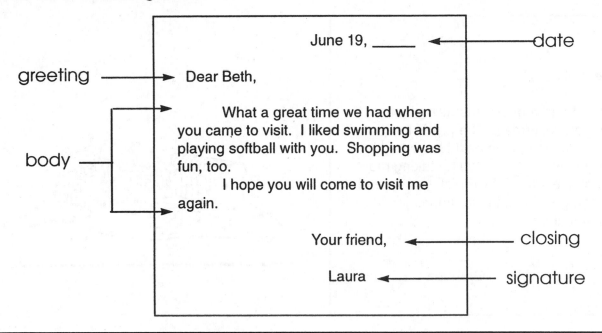

greeting

body

June 19, _____ ← date

Dear Beth,

     What a great time we had when you came to visit. I liked swimming and playing softball with you. Shopping was fun, too.

     I hope you will come to visit me again.

Your friend, ← closing

Laura ← signature

2. Answer Laura's letter. Talk about things you enjoyed during her visit.

_____
(date)

_____
(greeting)

_____

(body)

_____
(closing)

_____
(signature)

| A friendly letter has 5 parts: date, greeting, body, closing, and signature. |

1. Read the following letter.

August 6, _____

Dear Mike,

     I had a good time riding bikes with you yesterday. The picnic lunch you packed was the best I have had in many years. Thank you for taking me along! Next week I will pick you up and we can go fishing in the mountains. See you then.

Love,

Grandpa

2. Write a letter to Grandpa. Talk about what you will bring on the fishing trip.

_____
(date)

_____
(greeting)

_____

_____

_____

_____

_____
(body)

_____
(closing)

_____
(signature)

A friendly letter has 5 parts: date, greeting, body, closing, and signature.

1. Read the following letter.

> September 5, ____
>
> Dear Aaron,
>
> School has started again and I think I will like 4th grade. My teacher is pretty nice and we do not have a lot of homework (most of the time). Best of all, we are going to study Egypt this year! Remember that Sphinx we made on the beach last summer? Now I will learn how they were really made!
>
> Write soon,
>
> Meyer

2. Write a letter to Aaron. Talk about things that are happening in your class.

_____
(date)

_____
(greeting)

_____

_____

_____

_____

_____
(body)

_____

_____
(closing)

_____
(signature)

| A friendly letter has 5 parts: date, greeting, body, closing, and signature. |

1. Write a letter to your aunt. Thank her for the book she sent you. Include all 5 parts of a letter. Be sure to put a comma after the greeting and closing.

_____

_____

_____

_____

_____

_____

_____

_____

_____

2. Write a letter to your grandmother. Ask her to send you some of her special chocolate chip cookies. Include all 5 parts of a letter. Be sure to put a comma after the greeting and closing.

_____

_____

_____

_____

_____

_____

_____

_____

_____

| A friendly letter has 5 parts: date, greeting, body, closing, and signature. |

1. Write a letter to your Mayor. Tell him/her what is good about your city. Include all 5 parts of a letter. Be sure to put a comma after the greeting and closing.

_____

_____

_____

_____

_____

_____

_____

_____

_____

2. Write a letter to your mom or dad. Tell they why you like being their child. Include all 5 parts of a letter. Be sure to put a comma after the greeting and closing.

_____

_____

_____

_____

_____

_____

_____

_____

_____

| A friendly letter has 5 parts: date, greeting, body, closing, and signature. |

1. Write a letter to your favorite TV star. Think of things you would like to ask.
Include all 5 parts of a letter with commas after the greeting and closing.

_____
_____
_____
_____
_____
_____
_____
_____
_____

2. Write a letter to your favorite author telling what you liked about his/her
book.   Include all 5 parts of a letter with commas after the greeting and
closing.

_____
_____
_____
_____
_____
_____
_____
_____
_____

A friendly letter has 5 parts: date, greeting, body, closing, and signature.

Write a letter to one of your friends.

Describe yourself.

Tell what you like to do.

Describe your room.

Describe your family.

A Paragraph contains a main idea and supporting details.

Every paragraph has one main idea. The main idea is called the **topic sentence**. It is usually the first sentence in the paragraph. The other sentences are **details** that tell more about the main idea. The last sentence retells the main idea.

---

1. Read the title, main idea, and details listed below.

Title of paragraph: <u>My Teacher</u>

Main Idea: Mrs. Black is the best math teacher I have ever had.

Details: 1. She explains math so I can understand.
                    2. She always answers my questions when I need help.
                    3. She gives just the right amount of homework.
                    4. She reviews the chapter before a test.

Retell Main Idea: Mrs. Black is my favorite teacher.

---

2. Use the information to write a paragraph. Include the main idea and details then retell the main idea. Indent the first sentence. Use capitals and periods. Remember to give the paragraph a title.

_____

_____

_____

_____

_____

_____

_____

_____

_____

A Paragraph contains a main idea and supporting details.

Every paragraph has one main idea. The main idea is called the **topic sentence**. It is usually the first sentence in the paragraph. The other sentences are **details** that tell more about the main idea. The last sentence retells the main idea.

1. Read the title, main idea and details listed below.

Title of paragraph: <u>Soup for Dinner</u>

Main Idea: When mom lets me make dinner, I like to make soup.

Details: 1. I open the can carefully and pour the soup into a pot.
                          2. I fill the can with water and add that to the pot.
                          3. I stir it well while it is heating.
                          4. I put the soup in bowls and add crackers.

Retell Main Idea: Soup makes a wonderful dinner!

2. Use the information to write a paragraph. Include the main idea and details then retell the main idea. Indent the first sentence. Use capitals and periods. Remember to give the paragraph a title.

_____

_____

_____

_____

_____

_____

_____

_____

_____

_____

A Paragraph contains a main idea and supporting details.

Every paragraph has one main idea. The main idea is called the **topic sentence**. It is usually the first sentence in the paragraph. The other sentences are **details** that tell more about the main idea. The last sentence retells the main idea.

1. Read the title and main idea of the paragraph. Write your own details.

Title of paragraph:　　　　　　　<u>My Best Friend</u>

Main Idea:　　　　　　　My best friend is someone special.

Details:　　　　　　　1. _____
　　　　　　　　　　　2. _____
　　　　　　　　　　　3. _____
　　　　　　　　　　　4. _____

Retell Main Idea:　　　　　　　I am glad I have such a great friend.

2. Use the information to write a paragraph. Include the main idea and details then retell the main idea. Indent the first sentence. Use capitals and periods. Remember to give the paragraph a title.

_____

_____

_____

_____

_____

_____

_____

_____

_____

A Paragraph contains a main idea and supporting details.

Every paragraph has one main idea. The main idea is called the **topic sentence**. It is usually the first sentence in the paragraph. The other sentences are **details** that tell more about the main idea. The last sentence retells the main idea.

1. Read the title and main idea of the paragraph. Write your own details.

Title of paragraph: <u>School</u>

Main Idea: School helps me learn new things.

Details: 1. _____
                          2. _____
                          3. _____
                          4. _____

Retell Main Idea: School is a good place to learn.

2. Use the information to write a paragraph. Include the main idea and details then retell the main idea. Indent the first sentence. Use capitals and periods. Remember to give the paragraph a title.

_____

_____

_____

_____

_____

_____

_____

_____

_____

_____

A Paragraph contains a main idea and supporting details.

Every paragraph has one main idea. The main idea is called the **topic sentence**. It is usually the first sentence in the paragraph. The other sentences are **details** that tell more about the main idea. The last sentence retells the main idea.

1. Read the title and main idea of the paragraph. Write your own details.

Title of paragraph: <u>My Favorite Holiday</u>

Main Idea: My favorite holiday is _____

Details: 1. _____
                      2. _____
                      3. _____
                      4. _____

Retell Main Idea: _____ will always be the best!

2. Use the information to write a paragraph. Include the main idea and details then retell the main idea. Indent the first sentence. Use capitals and periods. Remember to give the paragraph a title.

_____

_____

_____

_____

_____

_____

_____

_____

_____

A Paragraph contains a main idea and supporting details.

Every paragraph has one main idea. The main idea is called the **topic sentence**. It is usually the first sentence in the paragraph. The other sentences are **details** that tell more about the main idea. The last sentence retells the main idea.

1. Choose an idea for your paragraph. Write the title, main idea, and details. Retell the main idea at the end.

Title of paragraph: _____

Main Idea: _____

Details:
1. _____
2. _____
3. _____
4. _____

Retell Main Idea: _____

2. Use the information to write a paragraph. Include the main idea and details then retell the main idea. Indent the first sentence. Use capitals and periods. Remember to give the paragraph a title.

_____

_____

_____

_____

_____

_____

_____

_____

_____

A Paragraph contains a main idea and supporting details.

Some paragraphs are written to persuade, or change the way people think. These paragraphs have a main idea and supporting details.

1. **You must convince your friend to let you borrow her new shirt. Ask her, give your reasons, then ask again.**

Title :   The New Shirt

Main Idea: May I wear your new shirt to school?

Details: 1. It matches my pants so well.
                                      2. It fits me just right.
                                      3. The shirt is a good color on me.
                                      4. I will hang it up in the closet when I get home.

Ask again: Please let me borrow your new shirt today.

2. **Use the information to write a paragraph. Include the main idea and details then retell the main idea. Indent the first sentence. Use capitals and periods. Remember to give the paragraph a title.**

_____

_____

_____

_____

_____

_____

_____

_____

_____

A Paragraph contains a main idea and supporting details.

Some paragraphs are written to persuade, or change the way people think. These paragraphs have a main idea and supporting details.

---

1. You must convince your dad to let you have a pet bird. Ask him, give your reasons, then ask again.

Title :   The Bird

Main Idea: May I have a bird for a pet?

Details: 1. I will keep it in a cage on the porch.
                                  2. A bird is quiet and will never bark at night.
                                  3. Cleaning the cage is easy so I will do it every day.
                                  4. I am old enough to take good care of a pet.

Ask again: Wouldn't a bird make a great pet for me?

---

2. Use the information to write a paragraph. Include the main idea and details then retell the main idea. Indent the first sentence. Use capitals and periods. Remember to give the paragraph a title.

_____

_____

_____

_____

_____

_____

_____

_____

_____

_____

A Paragraph contains a main idea and supporting details.

Some paragraphs are written to persuade, or change the way people think. These paragraphs have a main idea and supporting details.

1. You must convince your dad to let you use his tools to fix your bike. Ask him, give your reasons, then ask again.

Title :   Dad's Tools

Main Idea: May I use your tools to fix my bike?

Details: 1. I will keep them in tool box next to my bike while I work.
                     2. The bike cannot be fixed without tools.
                     3. _____
                     4. _____

Ask again: _____

2. Use the information to write a paragraph. Include the main idea and details then retell the main idea. Indent the first sentence. Use capitals and periods. Remember to give the paragraph a title.

_____

_____

_____

_____

_____

_____

_____

_____

_____

A Paragraph contains a main idea and supporting details.

Some paragraphs are written to persuade, or change the way people think. These paragraphs have a main idea and supporting details.

---

1. You must convince your brother to let you play his video game. Ask him, give your reasons, then ask again.

Title :   Let's Play!

Main Idea: May I play your video game?

Details: 1. I will be very careful with it.
                                2. You can play the game with me.
                                3. _____
                                4. _____

Ask again: _____

---

2. Use the information to write a paragraph. Include the main idea and details then retell the main idea. Indent the first sentence. Use capitals and periods. Remember to give the paragraph a title.

_____

_____

_____

_____

_____

_____

_____

_____

_____

_____

A Paragraph contains a main idea and supporting details.

Some paragraphs are written to persuade, or change the way people think. These paragraphs have a main idea and supporting details.

1. You must convince your mom to let you go bowling. Ask her, give your reasons, then ask again.

Title :   _____

Main Idea: May I _____

Details: 1. _____
                      2. _____
                      3. _____
                      4. _____

Ask again: _____

2. Use the information to write a paragraph. Include the main idea and details then retell the main idea. Indent the first sentence. Use capitals and periods. Remember to give the paragraph a title.

_____

_____

_____

_____

_____

_____

_____

_____

_____

_____

A Paragraph contains a main idea and supporting details.

Some paragraphs are written to persuade, or change the way people think. These paragraphs have a main idea and supporting details.

1. Ask your mother's permission for something. Give your reasons why you should be given permission, then ask again.

_____

Title : _____

Main Idea: May I _____

Details: 1. _____
                  2. _____
                  3. _____
                  4. _____

Ask again: _____

2. Use the information to write a paragraph. Include the main idea and details then retell the main idea. Indent the first sentence. Use capitals and periods. Remember to give the paragraph a title.

_____

_____

_____

_____

_____

_____

_____

_____

_____

_____

Some things can be both alike and different.

1. Complete the circles by comparing and contrasting a balloon and a baseball.

balloon   baseball

contrast	compare	contrast
1. pops easily	1. round	1. hard covering
2. stretchy	2. play with it	2. used in sports
3. _____	3. _____	3. _____

2. Write 2 paragraphs below. In the first paragraph tell how balloons and baseballs are alike. Tell how each is different in the second paragraph. Indent the first sentence. Title your story.

_____

_____

_____

_____

_____

_____

_____

_____

_____

_____

_____

Some things can be both alike and different.

1. Complete the circles by comparing and contrasting a school and an office.

school   office

contrast	compare	contrast
1. place to learn	1. has desks	1. place to work
2. has a principal	2. is a building	2. has a boss
3. _____	3. _____	3. _____

2. Write 2 paragraphs below. In the first paragraph tell how a school and an office are alike. Tell how each is different in the second paragraph. Indent the first sentence. Title your story.

_____

_____

_____

_____

_____

_____

_____

_____

_____

_____

Some things can be both alike and different.

1. **Complete the circles by comparing and contrasting a newspaper and a book.**

newspaper   _book_

contrast	compare	contrast
1. large pages	1. has stories	1. small pages
2. _____	2. _____	2. _____
3. _____	3. _____	3. _____

2. **Write 2 paragraphs below. In the first paragraph tell how newspapers and books are alike. Tell how each is different in the second paragraph. Indent the first sentence. Title your story.**

_____

_____

_____

_____

_____

_____

_____

_____

_____

_____

_____

_____

Name ________________________________ Skill: Compare and Contrast

Some things can be both alike and different.

1. Complete the circles by comparing and contrasting skating to riding a bike.

	skating		bike riding	

contrast	compare	contrast
1. put skates on	1. move quickly	1. sit on a seat
2. ______________	2. ______________	2. ______________
3. ______________	3. ______________	3. ______________

2. Write 2 paragraphs below. In the first paragraph tell how skating and riding bikes are alike. Tell how each is different in the second paragraph. Indent the first sentence. Title your story.

____

____

____

____

____

____

____

____

____

____

____

____

Some things can be both alike and different.

1. Complete the circles by comparing and contrasting yourself and a friend.

<u>yourself</u>   <u>friend</u>

contrast	compare	contrast
1. _____	1. _____	1. _____
2. _____	2. _____	2. _____
3. _____	3. _____	3. _____

2. Write 2 paragraphs below. In the first paragraph tell how you and your friend are alike. Tell how the two of you are different in the second paragraph. Indent the first sentence. Title your story.

_____

_____

_____

_____

_____

_____

_____

_____

_____

_____

_____

Some things can be both alike and different.

1. Choose your own topic to compare and contrast.

_____   _____

different	alike	different
1. _____	1. _____	1. _____
2. _____	2. _____	2. _____
3. _____	3. _____	3. _____

2. Write 2 paragraphs below. In the first paragraph tell how these two things are alike. Tell how each is different in the second paragraph. Indent the first sentence. Title your story.

_____

_____

_____

_____

_____

_____

_____

_____

_____

_____

_____

_____

Adjectives are words that describe which, how many, what color, and what an object looks or feels like. Adjectives make stories more colorful and interesting. They help you "see" a story in your imagination.

Here are 5 adjectives that describe each picture. Write a paragraph about each picture using these adjectives. Write a title for your paragraph.

1. crisp   2. juicy

3. red and green   4. tart

5. yummy

_____

_____

_____

_____

_____

_____

_____

1. bright   2. yellow

3. hot   4. high

5. far

_____

_____

_____

_____

_____

_____

Adjectives are words that describe which, how many, what color, and what an object looks or feels like. Adjectives make stories more colorful and interesting. They help you "see" a story in your imagination.

Here are 4 adjectives that describe each picture. Add an adjective of your own. Write a paragraph about each picture using these adjectives. Write a title for your paragraph.

1. frisky   2. floppy

3. wiggly   4. cuddly

5. _____

_____

_____
_____
_____
_____
_____
_____
_____
_____

1. white   2. far

3. fluffy   4. soft

5. _____

_____

_____
_____
_____
_____
_____
_____

Adjectives are words that describe which, how many, what color, and what an object looks or feels like. Adjectives make stories more colorful and interesting. They help you "see" a story in your imagination.

Here are 3 adjectives that describe each pictures. Add 2 adjectives of your own. Write a paragraph about each picture using these adjectives. Write a title for your paragraph.

1. sizzling

2. gooey

3. spicy

4. _____

5. _____

_____

_____

_____

_____

_____

_____

1. cold

2. sweet

3. wet

4. _____

5. _____

_____

_____

_____

_____

_____

_____

Adjectives are words that describe which, how many, what color, and what an object looks or feels like. Adjectives make stories more colorful and interesting. They help you "see" a story in your imagination.

Here are 2 adjectives that describe each picture. Add 3 adjectives of your own. Write a paragraph about each picture using these adjectives. Write a title for your paragraph.

1. interesting   2. colorful

3. _____ 4. _____

5. _____

_____

_____

_____

_____

_____

_____

1. round   2. black

3. _____ 4. _____

5. _____

_____

_____

_____

_____

_____

_____

Adjectives are words that describe which, how many, what color, and what an object looks or feels like. Adjectives make stories more colorful and interesting. They help you "see" a story in your imagination.

Draw or paste a picture in each box then write 5 adjectives that describe each picture. Write a paragraph about each picture using these adjectives. Give each story a title.

1. _____   2. _____

3. _____   4. _____

5. _____

_____

_____

_____

_____

_____

_____

1. _____   2. _____

3. _____   4. _____

5. _____

_____

_____

_____

_____

_____

_____

Adjectives are words that describe which, how many, what color, and what an object looks or feels like. Adjectives make stories more colorful and interesting. They help you "see" a story in your imagination.

1. Read this paragraph.

It was a nice day. Without warning, a storm suddenly blew in over the lake. We were afraid our boat would sink.

Here are some adjectives that help describe the sentences:

What kind of day it was : Bright, sunny, lovely, warm, spring
How the storm came in: quickly, gusting, swirling, howling, thundering, booming
What the storm looked like: dark, cloudy, windy, blackness, inky
What the people looked like: pale, tense, worried, frightened

2. Make the paragraph more interesting. Use the adjectives above or create your own to "draw a picture with words" of what has happened in the para- graph. Give the story a title.

_____

_____

_____

_____

_____

_____

_____

_____

_____

_____

_____

Adjectives are words that describe which, how many, what color, and what an object looks or feels like. Adjectives make stories more colorful and interesting. They help you "see" a story in your imagination.

1. Read this paragraph.

The old truck sat in the driveway. Dad and Sam were working on it. When the they finished, the truck would be as good as new.

Here are some adjectives that help describe the sentences:
   What the truck looked like: old, dented , faded green, rusty grey, dull,
       dented bumpers falling off
   How Dad and Sam were working: hard, difficult job, slowly, patiently
   How the truck would look in the end: shiny, glossy, bright, new

2. Make the paragraph more interesting. Use the adjectives above or create your own to "draw a picture with words" of what has happened in the paragraph. Give the story a title.

_____

_____

_____

_____

_____

_____

_____

_____

_____

_____

_____

> Adjectives are words that describe which, how many, what color, and what an object looks or feels like. Adjectives make stories more colorful and interesting. They help you "see" a story in your imagination.

1. Read this paragraph.

   The Christmas tree was nicely decorated. A star was on the top. There were lots of presents under the tree.

Here are some adjectives that help describe the sentences:

How the tree looked: beautiful, red and silver, twinkling, sparkling, colorful, prickly, golden, shining

How the presents looked: lovely, green and gold, bright bows, inviting

---

2. Make the paragraph more interesting. Use the adjectives above or create your own to "draw a picture with words" of what has happened in the paragraph. Give the story a title.

_____

_____

_____

_____

_____

_____

_____

_____

_____

_____

_____

Adjectives are words that describe which, how many, what color, and what an object looks or feels like. Adjectives make stories more colorful and interesting. They help you "see" a story in your imagination.

Read the sentence below. Write adjectives in the work box to add description to the sentence. Use the adjectives to write an interesting paragraph. Give the paragraph a title.

The house on the hill looked frightening.

What did the house look like? _____
_____
_____

What made it frightening? _____
_____
_____

_____

_____
_____
_____
_____
_____
_____
_____
_____
_____
_____

Adjectives are words that describe which, how many, what color, and what an object looks or feels like. Adjectives make stories more colorful and interesting. They help you "see" a story in your imagination.

Read the sentence below. Write adjectives in the work box to add description to the sentence. Use the adjectives to write an interesting paragraph. Give the paragraph a title.

My room is really a mess.

What makes your room a mess?_____
_____
_____

What words describe the mess?_____
_____
_____

_____

_____

_____

_____

_____

_____

_____

_____

_____

_____

Stories have a beginning, a middle, and an end.

1. Make up your own story by answering the questions about the picture. Use adjectives for description. Write complete sentences.

1. Who or what is this story about? _____
_____
_____

2. Where does this story take place? _____
_____
_____

3. How does this story begin? _____
_____
_____

4. What will happen next? _____
_____

5. How will the story end? _____
_____

2. Write a story using your sentences. Be sure to use capitals and periods. Remember to indent the first line. Title your story.

_____

_____
_____
_____
_____
_____
_____
_____

Stories have a beginning, a middle, and an end.

1. Make up your own story by answering the questions about the picture. Use adjectives for description. Write complete sentences.

1. Who or what is this story about? _____
_____
_____

2. Where does this story take place? _____
_____
_____

3. How does this story begin? _____
_____
_____

4. What will happen next? _____
_____

5. How will the story end? _____
_____

2. Write a story using your sentences. Be sure to use capitals and periods. Remember to indent the first line. Title your story.

_____

_____
_____
_____
_____
_____
_____
_____
_____
_____

Stories have a beginning, a middle, and an end.

1. Make up your own story by answering the questions about the picture. Use adjectives for description. Write complete sentences.

1. Who or what is this story about? _____
   _____
   _____

2. Where does this story take place? _____
   _____
   _____

3. How does this story begin? _____
   _____
   _____

4. What will happen next? _____
   _____

5. How will the story end? _____
   _____

2. Write a story using your sentences. Be sure to use capitals and periods. Remember to indent the first line. Title your story.

_____

_____

_____

_____

_____

_____

_____

_____

_____

Stories have a beginning, a middle, and an end.

1. Make up your own story by answering the questions about the picture. Use adjectives for description. Write complete sentences.

1. Who or what is this story about? _____
_____
_____

2. Where does this story take place? _____
_____
_____

3. How does this story begin? _____
_____
_____

4. What will happen next? _____
_____

5. How will the story end? _____
_____

2. Write a story using your sentences. Be sure to use capitals and periods. Remember to indent the first line. Title your story.

_____

_____
_____
_____
_____
_____
_____
_____
_____

Stories have a beginning, a middle, and an end.

1. Make up your own story by answering the questions about the picture. Use adjectives for description. Write complete sentences.

1. Who or what is this story about? _____
_____
_____

2. Where does this story take place? _____
_____
_____

3. How does this story begin? _____
_____
_____

4. What will happen next? _____
_____

5. How will the story end? _____
_____

2. Write a story using your sentences. Be sure to use capitals and periods. Remember to indent the first line. Title your story.

_____

_____
_____
_____
_____
_____
_____
_____
_____

Stories have a beginning, a middle, and an end.

Write 3 more words about the picture in the word box. Use the words to write a story. Be sure to use adjectives, capitals, and periods. Title your story.

THINGS TO THINK ABOUT
Who is this story about? Where does this story take place? How does this story begin? What happens next? How will you make this story end?

Word Box

girl	tired
yawning	_____
sleepy	_____
pillow	_____

_____

_____

_____

_____

_____

_____

_____

_____

_____

_____

Stories have a beginning, a middle, and an end.

Write 4 more words about the picture in the word box. Use the words to write a story. Be sure to use adjectives, capitals, and periods. Title your story.

THINGS TO THINK ABOUT
Who is this story about? Where does this story take place? How does this story begin? What happens next? How will you make this story end?

Word Box

boys	_____
grass	_____
trucks	_____
happy	_____

_____

_____

_____

_____

_____

_____

_____

_____

_____

Stories have a beginning, a middle, and an end.

Write 5 more words about the picture in the word box. Use the words to write a story. Be sure to use adjectives, capitals, and periods. Title your story.

THINGS TO THINK ABOUT
Who is this story about? Where does this story take place? How does this story begin? What happens next? How will you make this story end?

Word Box

bed   _____

sleeping   _____

blanket   _____

_____ _____

Stories have a beginning, a middle, and an end.

Write 6 more words about the picture in the word box. Use the words to write a story. Be sure to use adjectives, capitals, and periods. Title your story.

THINGS TO THINK ABOUT
Who is this story about? Where does this story take place? How does this story begin? What happens next? How will you make this story end?

Word Box

ocean   _____

fish   _____

_____   _____

_____   _____

_____

_____

_____

_____

_____

_____

_____

_____

_____

_____

_____

Stories have a beginning, a middle, and an end.

Write 8 words about the picture in the word box. Use the words to write a story.
Be sure to use adjectives, capitals, and periods. Title your story.

THINGS TO THINK ABOUT
Who is this story about? Where does this story take place? How does
this story begin? What happens next? How will you make this story end?

Word Box

_____

_____

_____

_____

_____

_____

_____

_____

_____

_____

_____

_____

Stories have a beginning, a middle, and an end.

Use the words in the web to write a story about the picture.
Be sure to use capitals and periods. Title your story.

THINGS TO THINK ABOUT
Who is this story about? Where does this story take place? How does this story begin? What happens next? How will you make this story end?

_____

_____

_____

_____

_____

_____

_____

_____

_____

_____

_____

Stories have a beginning, a middle, and an end.

Finish the story web. Use the words in the web to write a story about the picture. Be sure to use capitals and periods. Title your story.

THINGS TO THINK ABOUT
Who is this story about? Where does this story take place? How does this story begin? What happens next? How will you make this story end?

feet	space ship

trolley	transportation	bicycle

_____

_____

_____

_____

_____

_____

_____

_____

_____

_____

_____

_____

Stories have a beginning, a middle, and an end.

Finish the story web. Use the words in the web to write a story about the picture. Be sure to use capitals and periods. Title your story.

THINGS TO THINK ABOUT
Who is this story about? Where does this story take place? How does this story begin? What happens next? How will you make this story end?

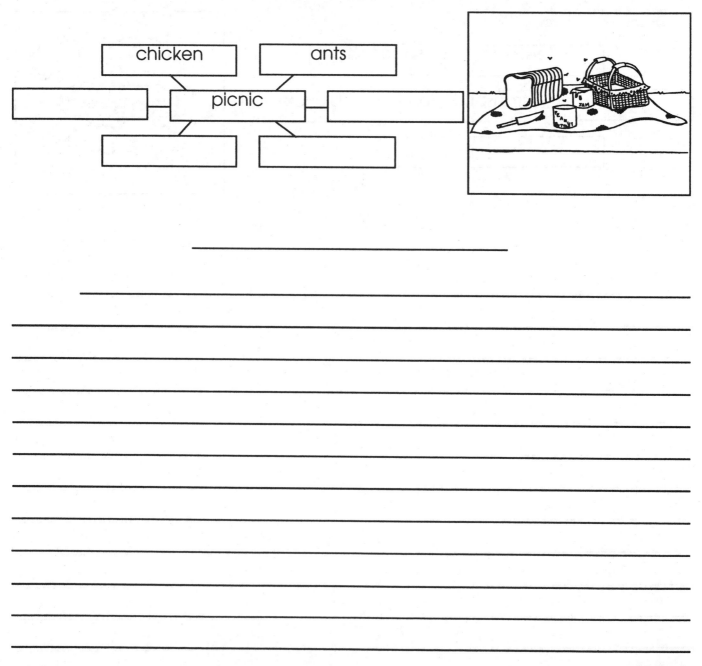

_____

_____

_____

_____

_____

_____

_____

_____

_____

_____

_____

_____

Stories have a beginning, a middle, and an end.

Finish the story web. Use the words in the web to write a story about the picture. Be sure to use capitals and periods. Title your story.

THINGS TO THINK ABOUT
Who is this story about? Where does this story take place? How does this story begin? What happens next? How will you make this story end?

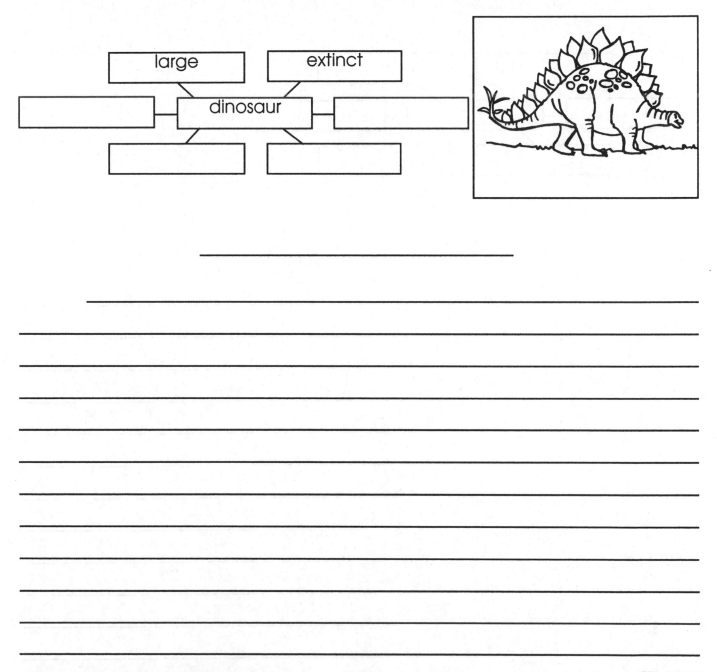

_____

_____

_____

_____

_____

_____

_____

_____

_____

_____

_____

_____

_____

Stories have a beginning, a middle, and an end.

Choose a topic and fill in the story web. Use the words in the web to write a story. Be sure to use capitals and periods. Title your story.

THINGS TO THINK ABOUT
Who is this story about? Where does this story take place? How does this story begin? What happens next? How will you make this story end?

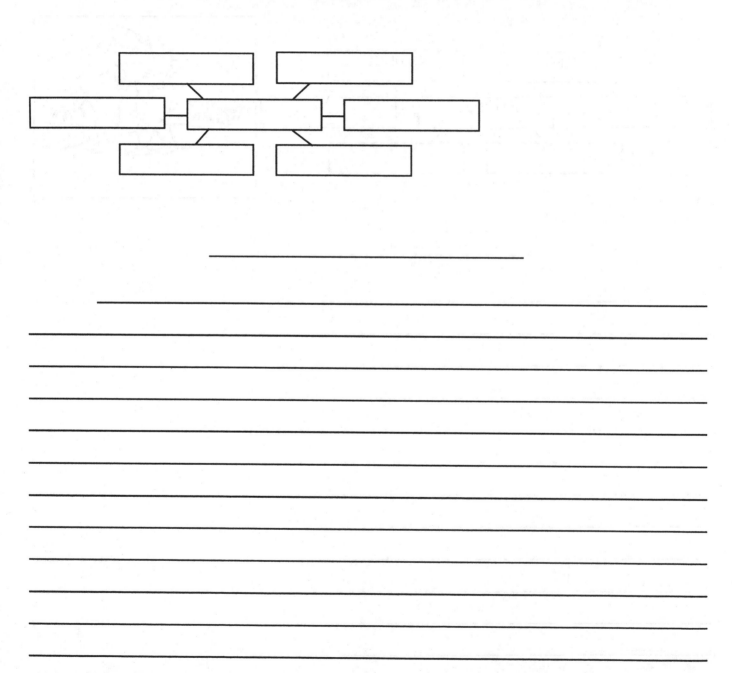

_____

_____

_____

_____

_____

_____

_____

_____

_____

_____

_____

_____

THINGS TO THINK ABOUT FOR EVERY STORY:

★ Sentences begin with capitals and end with periods, question marks, or exclamation marks.
★ A paragraph contains a main idea and supporting details.
★ The first sentence of a paragraph should be indented.
★ Adjectives make stories more colorful and interesting.
★ A story tells who did what, when and where it was done, how it happened, and why it happened.
★ Stories have a beginning, a middle, and an end.

Write a story about the picture below. Be sure to follow all the hints in the "Things to Think About" box. Give your story a title.

Name ______________________________ Skill: Writing Stories

THINGS TO THINK ABOUT FOR EVERY STORY:

- ★ Sentences begin with capitals and end with periods, question marks, or exclamation marks.
- ★ A paragraph contains a main idea and supporting details.
- ★ The first sentence of a paragraph should be indented.
- ★ Adjectives make stories more colorful and interesting.
- ★ A story tells who did what, when and where it was done, how it happened, and why it happened.
- ★ Stories have a beginning, a middle, and an end.

Write a story about the picture below. Be sure to follow all the hints in the "Things to Think About" box. Give your story a title.

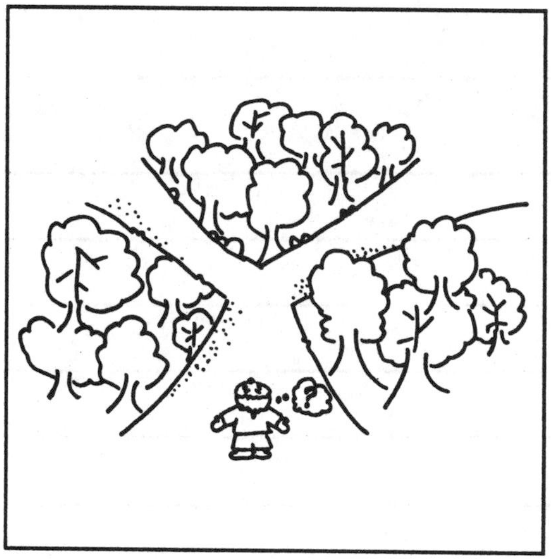

THINGS TO THINK ABOUT FOR EVERY STORY:

★ Sentences begin with capitals and end with periods, question marks, or exclamation marks.
★ A paragraph contains a main idea and supporting details.
★ The first sentence of a paragraph should be indented.
★ Adjectives make stories more colorful and interesting.
★ A story tells who did what, when and where it was done, how it hapened, and why it happened.
★ Stories have a beginning, a middle, and an end.

Write a story about the picture below. Be sure to follow all the hints in the "Things to Think About" box. Give your story a title.

Name ______________________________ Skill: Writing Stories

THINGS TO THINK ABOUT FOR EVERY STORY:

- ★ **Sentences begin with capitals and end with periods, question marks, or exclamation marks.**
- ★ **A paragraph contains a main idea and supporting details.**
- ★ **The first sentence of a paragraph should be indented.**
- ★ **Adjectives make stories more colorful and interesting.**
- ★ **A story tells who did what, when and where it was done, how it happened, and why it happened.**
- ★ **Stories have a beginning, a middle, and an end.**

Write a story about the picture below. Be sure to follow all the hints in the "Things to Think About" box. Give your story a title.

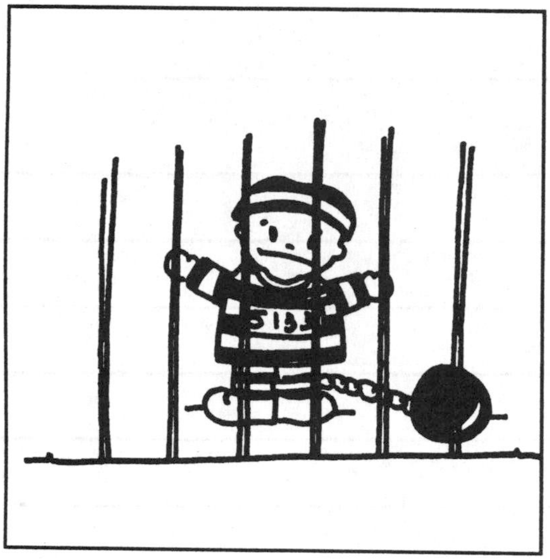

Name ______________________________ Skill: Writing Stories

THINGS TO THINK ABOUT FOR EVERY STORY:

★ Sentences begin with capitals and end with periods, question marks, or exclamation marks.
★ A paragraph contains a main idea and supporting details.
★ The first sentence of a paragraph should be indented.
★ Adjectives make stories more colorful and interesting.
★ A story tells who did what, when and where it was done, how it happened, and why it happened.
★ Stories have a beginning, a middle, and an end.

Write a story about the picture below. Be sure to follow all the hints in the "Things to Think About" box. Give your story a title.

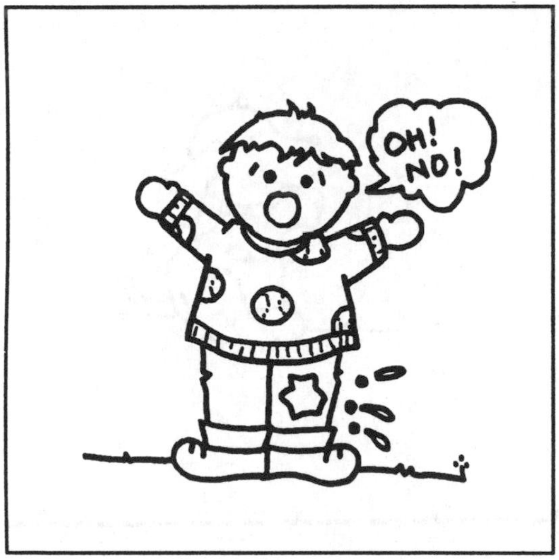

Putting Paragraphs Together

★ An opening paragraph gives the topic of the story. It should catch the interest of the reader.

★ The second paragraph gives more information about the topic of the story.

★ The last paragraph reviews the main idea and ends the story.

★ Each paragraph contains a main idea and supporting details.

Use the information contained in this outline to write a three paragraph story. Use an additional sheet of paper if you need more space.

Title: My Pet
Main Idea: I. New puppy
Details: A. Snaps at my heels
                         B. Named him Nip
                         C. Brown and White

Main Idea: II. Noisy and playful
                         A.   Barks all night
                         B.   Chewed up my shoes
                         C. Chases his tail

Main Idea: III. Love my puppy
                         A.   Train him
                         B.   Teach him tricks
                         C. We are best friends

Putting Paragraphs Together

★ An opening paragraph gives the topic of the story. It should catch the interest of the reader.
★ The second paragraph gives more information about the topic of the story.
★ The last paragraph reviews the main idea and ends the story.
★ Each paragraph contains a main idea and supporting details.

Complete the outline below. Use the information to write a three paragraph story. Add your own details. Use an additional sheet of paper if you need more space.

Title: The Terrible Storm
Main Idea: I.   Storm began to rage
Details: A. Wind began to blow
                       B. Thunder and lightening
                       C. _____

Main Idea: II. Power went out
                       A.   House went dark
                       B. Candles for light
                       C. _____

Main Idea: III. Great time
                       A.   Played hiding games
                       B. Told ghost stories
                       C. _____

_____

                    _____

_____

_____

_____

_____

_____

_____

_____

Putting Paragraphs Together

★ An opening paragraph gives the topic of the story. It should catch the interest of the reader.
★ The second paragraph gives more information about the topic of the story.
★ The last paragraph reviews the main idea and ends the story.
★ Each paragraph contains a main idea and supporting details.

Complete the outline below. Use the information to write a three paragraph story. Add your own details. Use an additional sheet of paper if you need more space.

Title: <u>The Accident</u>
Main Idea: I. Broke my leg
Details: A. Riding my bike
                    B. Big tree in my path
                    C. _____

Main Idea: II. Went to the hospital
                    A. Mom took me in the car
                    B. Doctor took x-rays
                    C. _____

Main Idea: III. Home at last
                    A. Walking on crutches
                    B. Cast signed by friends
                    C. _____

_____

          _____

_____

_____

_____

_____

_____

_____

_____

Putting Paragraphs Together

★ An opening paragraph gives the topic of the story. It should catch the interest of the reader.

★ The second paragraph gives more information about the topic of the story.

★ The last paragraph reviews the main idea and ends the story.

★ Each paragraph contains a main idea and supporting details.

Complete the outline below. Use the information to write a three paragraph story. Add your own details. Use an additional sheet of paper if you need more space.

Title: Where Are You?
Main Idea: I.   Lost my little sister
Details: A. Shopping at the clothing store
                         B. _____
                         C. _____

Main Idea: II. Looked Everywhere
                         A. Walked up and down every aisle
                         B. _____
                         C. _____

Main Idea: III. Finally found her
                         A. Saw her legs under the coats on the rack
                         B. _____
                         C. _____

_____

_____

_____

_____

_____

_____

_____

_____

_____

Putting Paragraphs Together
★ An opening paragraph gives the topic of the story. It should catch the interest of the reader.
★ The second paragraph gives more information about the topic of the story.
★ The last paragraph reviews the main idea and ends the story.
★ Each paragraph contains a main idea and supporting details.

Choose a topic and complete the outline below. Use the information to write a three paragraph story. Add your own details. Use an additional sheet of paper if you need more space.

Title: _____

Main Idea: I. _____

Details: A. _____
                     B. _____
                     C. _____

Main Idea: II. _____
                     A. _____
                     B. _____
                     C. _____

Main Idea: III. _____
                     A. _____
                     B. _____
                     C. _____

_____

_____

_____

_____

_____

_____

_____

_____

_____

Putting Paragraphs Together
An opening paragraph gives the topic of the story. It should catch the interest of the reader.
The second paragraph gives more information about the topic of the story.
The last paragraph reviews the main idea and ends the story.
Each paragraph contains a main idea and supporting details.

Use the information given in the story web to write a three paragraph story. Title the story. Use the back of this page if you need more space.

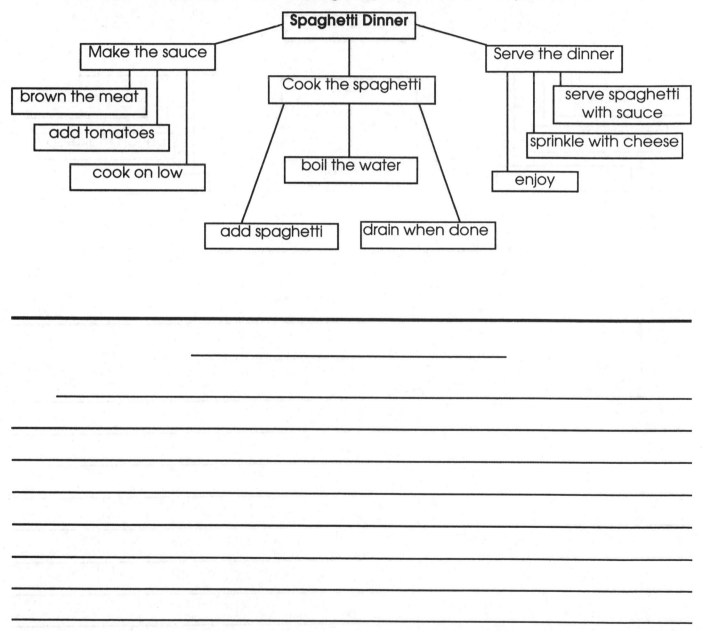

_____

_____

_____

_____

_____

_____

_____

_____

_____

Putting Paragraphs Together

An opening paragraph gives the topic of the story. It should catch the interest of the reader.

The second paragraph gives more information about the topic of the story.

The last paragraph reviews the main idea and ends the story.

Each paragraph contains a main idea and supporting details.

Use the information given in the story web to write a three paragraph story. Title the story. Use the back of this page if you need more space.

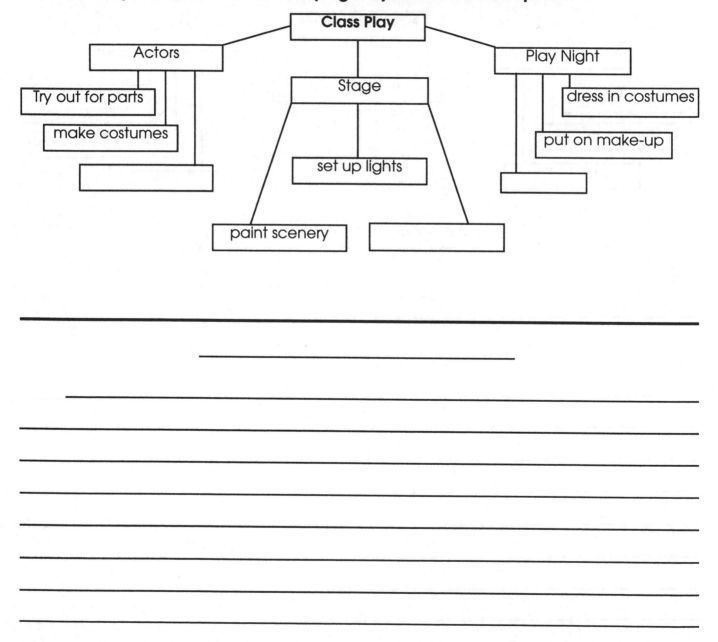

_____

                    _____

_____

_____

_____

_____

_____

_____

_____

Putting Paragraphs Together
An opening paragraph gives the topic of the story. It should catch the interest of the reader.
The second paragraph gives more information about the topic of the story.
The last paragraph reviews the main idea and ends the story.
Each paragraph contains a main idea and supporting details.

Use the information given in the story web to write a three paragraph story. Title the story. Use the back of this page if you need more space.

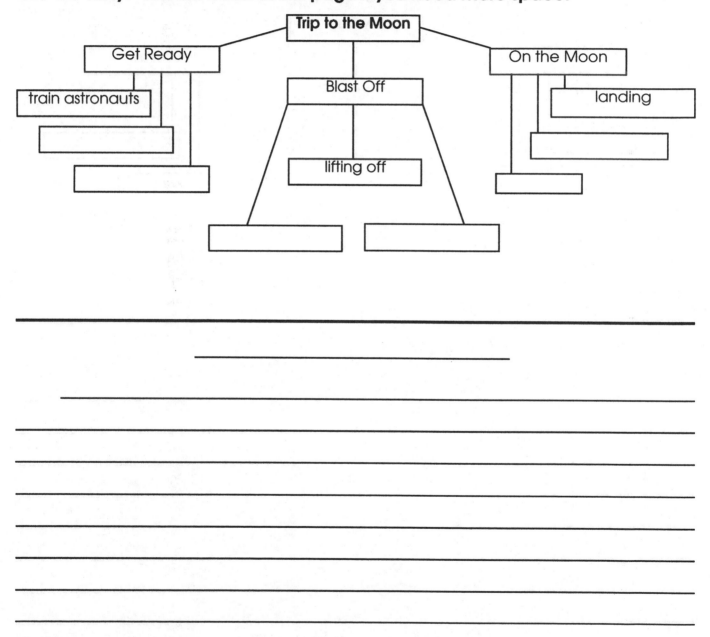

_____

_____

_____

_____

_____

_____

_____

_____

_____

Putting Paragraphs Together

An opening paragraph gives the topic of the story. It should catch the interest of the reader.

The second paragraph gives more information about the topic of the story.

The last paragraph reviews the main idea and ends the story.

Each paragraph contains a main idea and supporting details.

Use the information given in the story web to write a three paragraph story. Title the story. Use the back of this page if you need more space.

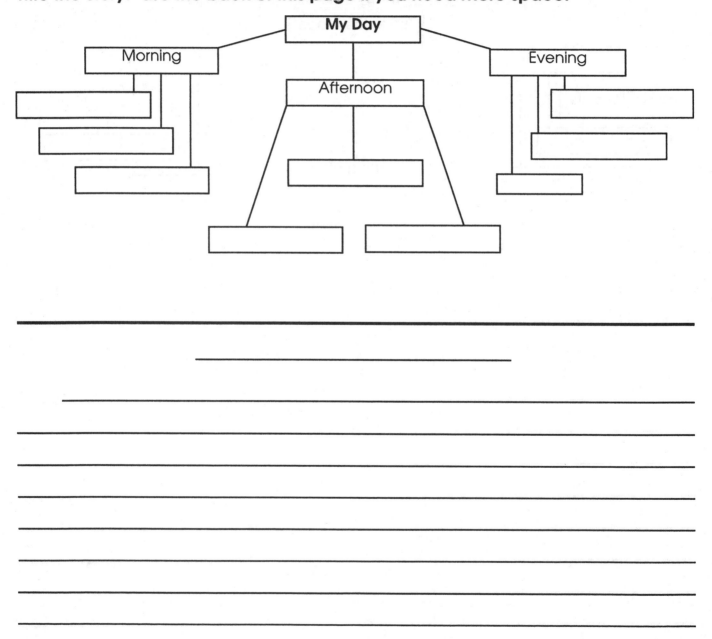

_____

_____

_____

_____

_____

_____

_____

_____

_____

Putting Paragraphs Together
An opening paragraph gives the topic of the story. It should catch the interest of the reader.
The second paragraph gives more information about the topic of the story.
The last paragraph reviews the main idea and ends the story.
Each paragraph contains a main idea and supporting details.

Choose a topic and complete the story web. Use it to write a three paragraph story. Use the back of this page if you need more space.

A report gives facts in an orderly and clear manner.

Use the information contained in this outline to write a report. Use the back of this page if you need more space.

Subject: Plants
Main Idea: I. Importance to Earth
Details: A. gives off oxygen
                  B. homes for many animals
                  C. beautiful to look at

Main Idea: II. Parts
                  A. roots
                  B. stems
                  C. leaves

Main Idea: III. Needs
                  A. air
                  B. water
                  C. sunlight

A report gives facts in an orderly and clear manner.

Use the information contained in this outline to write a report. Use the back of this page if you need more space.

Subject: Bodies of Water
Main Idea: I. Oceans
Details: A. salt water
                                      B. covers 75% of the Earth
                                      C. gives us food

Main Idea: II. Lakes
                                      A. mainly fresh water
                                      B. large body of water surrounded by land
                                      C. gives us drinking water and power

Main Idea: III. Needs
                                      A. fresh water
                                      B. large flowing stream of water
                                      C. gives us drinking water and power

_____

_____

_____

_____

_____

_____

_____

_____

_____

_____

_____

_____

A report gives facts in an orderly and clear manner.

Use the information contained in this outline to write a report. Use the back of this page if you need more space.

Subject: Doing Laundry
Main Idea: I. Sort Clothes
Details: A. whites
                             B. light colors
                             C. dark colors

Main Idea: II. Wash
                             A.   water temperature
                             B.   detergent
                             C.   load washer

Main Idea: III. Dry and Put Away
                             A.   temperature
                             B.   fold
                             C.   put away

_____

_____

_____

_____

_____

_____

_____

_____

_____

_____

_____

A report gives facts in an orderly and clear manner.

Use the information contained in this outline to write a report. Use the back of this page if you need more space.

Subject: Writing a Report
Main Idea: I.   Before Writing
Details: A. brainstorm for ideas
                            B. look up information
                            C. make an outline

Main Idea: II. Writing
                            A.   get information and materials together
                            B.   organize what you want to say
                            C.   write a first draft

Main Idea: III. Revise
                            A.   read to check facts and organization
                            B.   read to check spelling and punctuation
                            C.   rewrite neatly

_____

_____

_____

_____

_____

_____

_____

_____

_____

_____

_____

_____

A report gives facts in an orderly and clear manner.

Choose a topic and put the information in this outline. Write the report. Use the back of this page if you need more space.

Subject: _____

Main Idea: I. _____

Details:
    A. _____
    B. _____
    C. _____

Main Idea: II. _____
    A. _____
    B. _____
    C. _____

Main Idea: III. _____
    A. _____
    B. _____
    C. _____

_____

_____

_____

_____

_____

_____

_____

_____

_____

_____

_____

> The **first person point of view** tells a story as if the narrator were a part of it. This view uses the words "I", "me", or "we".
> The **third person point of view** tells the story as if the narrator were watching it happen. This view uses the words "he", "she", "they", or "them".

This story is written from the first person point of view. Rewrite the story, changing it to the third person point of view. Add your own ending.

A Skating Disaster

I was skating on the sidewalk a few blocks from my house yesterday afternoon when a dog darted out of the bushes. The dog ran right across my path. Boom, down I fell! I stood up and brushed myself off. Suddenly a little girl ran out of the same bushes. The girl was calling, "Come back, Pixie!" As she rushed past me, I fell down again. I had just picked myself up again when a man raced out of the bushes! He was shouting, "Come back, Terry! Come back, Pixie!" I.......

_____

_____

_____

_____

_____

_____

_____

_____

_____

_____

_____

_____

The **first person point of view** tells a story as if the narrator were a part of it. This view uses the words "I", "me", or "we".
The **third person point of view** tells the story as if the narrator were watching it happen. This view uses the words "he", "she", "they", or "them".

This story is written from the first person point of view. Rewrite the story, changing it to the third person point of view. Add your own ending.

<u>Guess Who</u>

Mysteries are my favorite type of book. When I start reading a mystery, I can't put the book down. I love to guess what will happen and try to solve the puzzle before I get to the ending. I get so caught up in the story that I forget all about time! Last night I began reading a mystery about a man who disappeared without a trace. It was such a good story that I didn't realize the time until the clock struck midnight. Suddenly.....

_____

_____

_____

_____

_____

_____

_____

_____

_____

_____

_____

> The **first person point of view** tells a story as if the narrator were a part of it. This view uses the words "I", "me", or "we".
> The **third person point of view** tells the story as if the narrator were watching it happen. This view uses the words "he", "she", "they", or "them".

This story is written from the first person point of view. Rewrite the story, changing it to the third person point of view. Add your own ending.

<u>A Fire in the Oven</u>

I am, without a doubt, the best chocolate chip cookie maker in the world. I measure just the right amount of flour, sugar, and salt. I mix these with butter, milk, and eggs. Then I add lots and lots of chocolate chips. Sometimes I take a little taste of the batter, and before I know it I have eaten half the cookie dough! Mmm, it is so good.

Last Saturday I had a little accident in the kitchen. I had just put the cookies in the oven to bake and the phone rang. I .....

_____

_____

_____

_____

_____

_____

_____

_____

_____

_____

_____

_____

_____

The **first person point of view** tells a story as if the narrator were a part of it. This view uses the words "I", "me", or "we".

The **third person point of view** tells the story as if the narrator were watching it happen. This view uses the words "he", "she", "they", or "them".

This story is written from the third person point of view. Rewrite the story, changing it to the first person point of view. Add your own ending.

Summer Camp

Last summer, Mark went to camp. He was gone for two weeks. He took his sleeping bag, flashlight, and bug spray. Mark camped in a cabin with three other boys. He made lots of new friends and learned many new things at camp. Every day he went swimming and he learned to paddle a canoe. Mark and his friends often went for hikes in the woods. Once they built a fire and cooked hotdogs and marshmallows over the flames. Mark.....

_____

_____

_____

_____

_____

_____

_____

_____

_____

_____

_____

_____

_____

The **first person point of view** tells a story as if the narrator were a part of it. This view uses the words "I", "me", or "we".
The **third person point of view** tells the story as if the narrator were watching it happen. This view uses the words "he", "she", "they", or "them".

This story is written from the third person point of view. Rewrite the story, changing it to the first person point of view. Add your own ending.

<u>Soccer Hero</u>

Joey has been playing soccer for three years. His team is called the Mountain Lions. Joey plays goalie on the team. A goalie tries to keep the other team from scoring by standing in front of the net and blocking any balls kicked toward it. Joey is a great goalie. He played on the "All Star Team" last year. Last Thursday the Mountain Lions played a team called the Blazing Suns. The Suns were ahead by two goals. The game was almost over and it looked like the Lions were going to lose. Joey...

_____

_____

_____

_____

_____

_____

_____

_____

_____

_____

_____

_____

_____

> **Sentences and proper nouns begin with capital letters.**
> **Sentences must have proper punctuation marks.**

Place capitals and punctuation marks in the proper places. Add an ending to the story.

<u>My Hollow Leg</u>

my mom says i have a hollow leg   she says my stomach is not big enough to hold all of the food that i eat   all that food has to go somewhere   it must be going down into my hollow leg

for breakfast this morning i ate six pancakes and five pieces of bacon   i was hungry long before noon   mom and i went to burger city for lunch   mom had a small hamburger but i had the burger blast special (a triple burger, double fries, and a large shake)   by 3:00 my stomach was growling again   i had to have something to eat   i had two peanut butter sandwiches and half an apple for a snack   i was really hungry by dinnertime

_____

_____

_____

_____

_____

_____

_____

_____

_____

> Sentences and proper nouns begin with capital letters.
> Sentences must have proper punctuation marks.

Place capitals and punctuation marks in the proper places. Add an ending to the story.

Creatures From Outer Space

tim and i decided to camp out in the back yard   we got our sleeping

bags two flashlights and some snacks   we unrolled our sleeping bags laid

down and began to munch on some pretzels   it was a clear night and the

stars were sparkling brightly   tim found the big dipper and the north star   one

bright star seemed to be moving   we watched it race across the sky

suddenly it stopped and began to grow bigger   it was coming toward us   it

came to a stop right over our heads   now we could see that it was not a star

at all   it was a spaceship a beam of light shot from the spaceship and

glowed all around tim

_____

_____

_____

_____

_____

_____

_____

_____

Sentences and proper nouns begin with capital letters.
Sentences must have proper punctuation marks.

Place capitals and punctuation marks in the proper places. Add an ending to the story.

<u>Lost in the Forest</u>

it was a lovely october day   beth and i took a walk in the woods to look

at the red gold and orange leaves   we were not alone in the woods

squirrels were busy gathering nuts for winter and deer were eating the last of

the green grass   the sky was filled with flocks of birds flying south to warmer

weather

just as we were turning to walk back beth spotted a small bear playing

under some trees   we crept closer to get a better look   the baby bear saw us

and cried out in fright   it began to run toward a large black rock   the black

rock began to move and actually stood up   it was not a rock at all   it was

the giant mother bear and she was angry

_____

_____

_____

_____

_____

_____

_____

_____

| Sentences and proper nouns begin with capital letters. |
| Sentences must have proper punctuation marks. |

Place capitals and punctuation marks in the proper places. Add an ending to the story.

My Fairy Godmother

penny was not very happy   it was her turn to do the dishes again and she hated that job   mother told penny that after the dishes were finished her room needed to be cleaned   penny grumbled to herself as she began to wash the dishes

it seemed like all she ever did in that house was clean or wash some thing   she was beginning to feel a little like cinderella   the only real difference was that she did not have a mean stepmother and she had no sisters at all   penny wished that she did have sisters   they could do all these dishes and clean her room for her   what a nice idea but she knew it was impossible to have wishes like that come true

a soft voice behind penny called her name   penny turned quickly and her mouth fell open in amazement

_____

_____

_____

_____

_____

_____

Name _____   Skill: Punctuation and Capitals

> **Sentences and proper nouns begin with capital letters.**
> **Sentences must have proper punctuation marks.**

Place capitals and punctuation marks in the proper places. Add an ending to the story.

Watermelon Seeds

mike's favorite food was watermelon   he ate it all summer long   he loved the sweet juicy taste   mike never wasted a bite   he didn t even mind the seeds   he would just swallow them whole as he gobbled down each large pink slice

uncle roy often warned mike about swallowing all those seeds   he told mike that the seeds would sprout in his stomach and grow into watermelons what would mike do then   mike would just laugh at the warnings

one hot afternoon mike ate three large slices of watermelon   he was about to have a fourth piece when he felt a strange rumbling in his stomach

_____

_____

_____

_____

_____

_____

_____

_____

_____

Actions tell us about characters.

Characters tell us about themselves by the way they act. These actions make something happen in a story. When we understand characters and their actions, we understand the story.

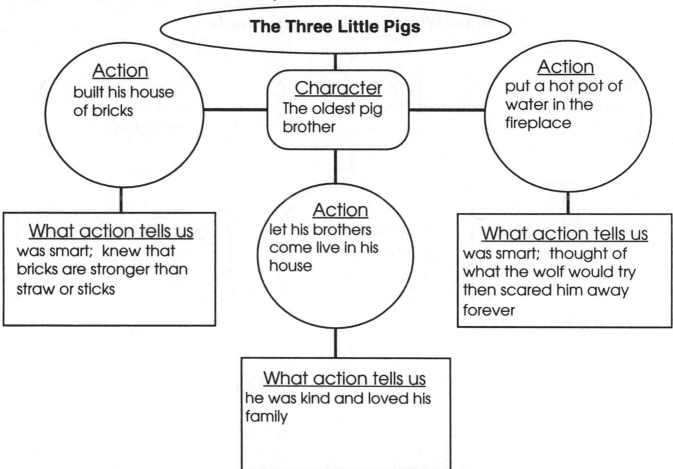

Use the information from the chart to write a paragraph about the oldest pig.

_____

_____

_____

_____

_____

_____

_____

Actions tell us about characters.

Characters tell us about themselves by the way they act. These actions make something happen in a story. When we understand characters and their actions, we understand the story.

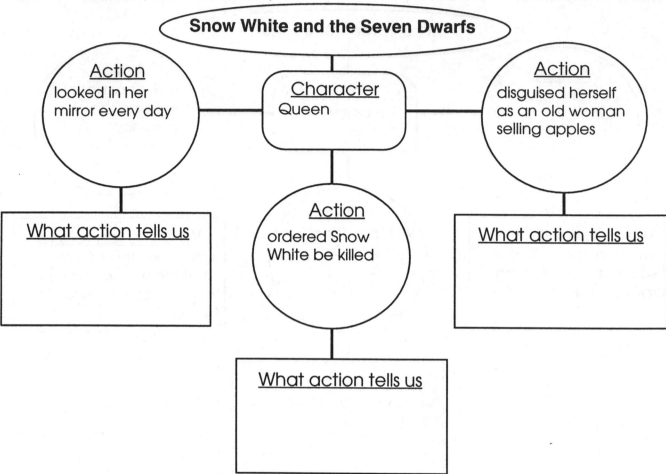

Snow White and the Seven Dwarfs

Action
looked in her
mirror every day

Character
Queen

Action
disguised herself
as an old woman
selling apples

What action tells us

Action
ordered Snow
White be killed

What action tells us

What action tells us

Complete the chart. Use the information to write a paragraph about the Queen.

_____

_____

_____

_____

_____

_____

_____

Actions tell us about characters.

Characters tell us about themselves by the way they act. These actions make something happen in a story. When we understand characters and their actions, we understand the story.

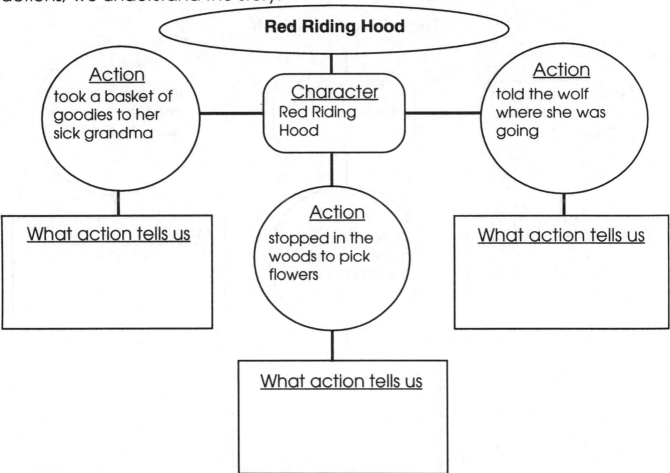

Complete the chart. Use the information to write a paragraph about Red Riding Hood.

_____

_____

_____

_____

_____

_____

Actions tell us about characters.

Characters tell us about themselves by the way they act. These actions make something happen in a story. When we understand characters and their actions, we understand the story.

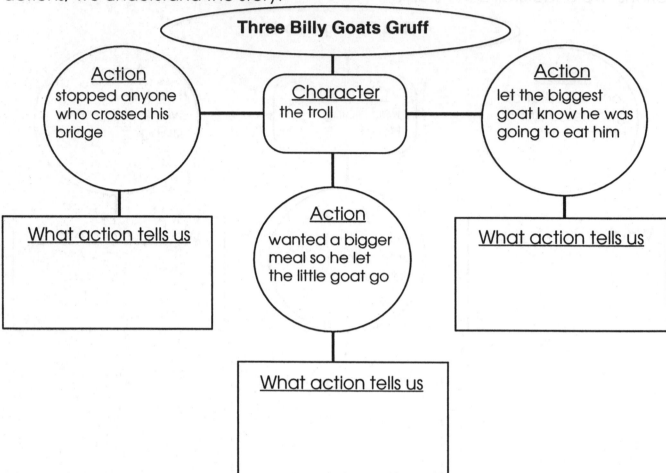

Three Billy Goats Gruff

Action
stopped anyone who crossed his bridge

Character
the troll

Action
let the biggest goat know he was going to eat him

What action tells us

Action
wanted a bigger meal so he let the little goat go

What action tells us

What action tells us

Complete the chart. Use the information to write a paragraph about the troll.

_____

_____

_____

_____

_____

_____

_____

Actions tell us about characters.

Characters tell us about themselves by the way they act. These actions make something happen in a story. When we understand characters and their actions, we understand the story.

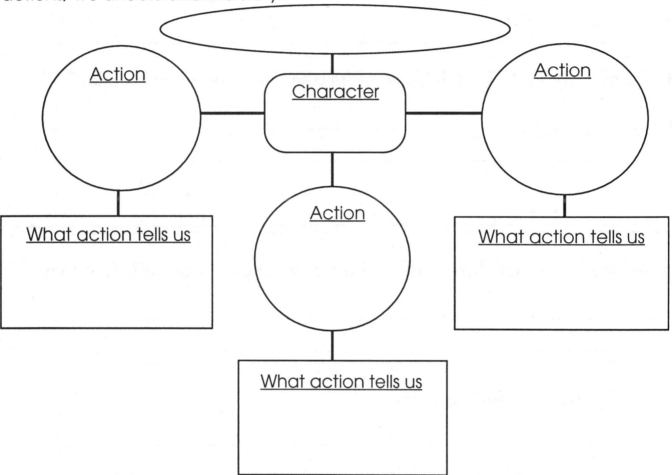

Complete the chart for a character from a story you have read. Use the information to write a paragraph about that character.

_____

_____

_____

_____

_____

_____

_____

Book Report

1. **Title:**

2. **Author:**

3. **Name 2 characters in this book. Write a sentence about each one.**

   1. _____   _____
      _____

   2. _____   _____
      _____

4. **Tell where this story takes place. Write a sentence to describe the setting.**

   _____

   _____

5. **What is the problem in this story?**

   _____

   _____

   _____

   _____

6. **How is the problem solved?**

   _____

   _____

   _____

   _____

Name _____

About This Book

Characters
_____
_____
_____

(title)
_____
By: _____
(author)

(beginning)

(middle)

(end)

Book Review

Title: _____

Author: _____

1. Retell the story in your own words. Be sure to include the characters, setting, beginning, middle, and end.

_____
_____
_____
_____
_____
_____
_____
_____
_____
_____

2. Tell what you liked most about this story. Tell why and give examples from the book.

_____
_____
_____
_____
_____
_____
_____
_____
_____

Book Report

Title: _____

Author: _____

Where did this story take place? _____

_____

1. Compare and contrast the main character with yourself.

_____   _____

   contrast   compare   compare

_____   _____   _____

_____   _____   _____

_____   _____   _____

_____   _____   _____

_____   _____   _____

_____   _____   _____

2. Tell what you liked or didn't like about the main character. Tell why and give examples from the book.

_____

_____

_____

_____

_____

_____

_____

_____

_____
(Title)

_____
(Author)

_____
(Date Published)

My favorite scene from the book.

WHO ? _____
_____

WHAT? _____
_____
_____
_____
_____

WHERE? _____
_____
_____

WHEN? _____

WHY? _____
_____
_____
_____
_____

Book Review

Title: _____

Author: _____

Date published: _____

Subject of the book: _____

Review of the book: _____

_____

_____

_____

_____

_____

_____

Interesting facts learned from this book: _____

_____

_____

_____

_____

_____

_____

_____

What I would like to know more about: _____

_____

_____

Who's in the News?

Title: _____

Author: _____

Date published: _____

Who this book is about: _____

Why is this person important? _____

_____

_____

_____

What interesting things did this person do? _____

_____

_____

_____

_____

_____

How did this person affect history? _____

_____

_____

_____

_____

_____

How do you feel about this person? Why? _____

_____

_____

_____

_____

_____

Writing Award

_____

receives this award for

_____

Keep up the great work!

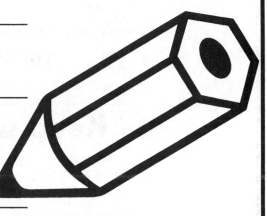

_____ _____
signed   date

Writing Whiz!

_____

receives this award for

_____

Great Job!

Great Job!

_____ _____
signed   date

Wonderful Writing!

_____

receives this award for

_____

Keep up the great work!

_____   _____
signed   date

All Star Writer

_____

is a Writing All Star!

_____

You are terrific!

_____   _____
signed   date

© 1996 Kelley Wingate Publications   CD-3719

Answer Key

© 1996 Kelley Wingate Publications   107   CD-3719

Worksheet 1

Name _____   Skill: Invitations

An invitation includes all the important facts.

"You are invited!" You must know <u>why</u>, <u>who</u>, <u>when</u>, and <u>where</u>. An invitation gives you all this information.

1. Read the invitation and answer the questions.

A CHRISTMAS PARTY!

Given by: Randy Johns
Time: 7:00 p.m.
Date: December 15
Place: 606 Lime Ave.

<u>Why</u> has the invitation been sent?
Christmas party
<u>Who</u> is giving the party?
Randy Johns
<u>When</u> will you go?
December 15 7:00 p.m.
<u>Where</u> will you go?
606 Lime Ave.

2. Write an invitation to a Going Away Party. List the important information and write the information on the invitation.

<u>Why</u> will the invitation be sent?
Goodbye party
<u>Who</u> is giving the party?
Answers will vary.
<u>When</u> is the party?
_____
<u>Where</u> is the party?

Come Say Goodbye
Given by: _____
Time: _____
Date: _____
Place: _____

©1996 Kelley Wingate Publications   1   KW 1204

Worksheet 2

Name _____   Skill: Invitations

An invitation includes all the important facts.

"You are invited!" You must know <u>why</u>, <u>who</u>, <u>when</u>, and <u>where</u>. An invitation gives you all this information.

1. Read the invitation and answer the questions.

Grand Opening: Jerry's Jeans Shop

Given by: Jerry Adams
Time: 10:00 a.m.
Date: August 17
Place: Lakeland Mall

<u>Why</u> has the invitation been sent?
Shop Opening
<u>Who</u> is giving the party?
Jerry Adams
<u>When</u> will you go?
August 17 10:00 a.m.
<u>Where</u> will you go?
Lakeland Mall

2. Write an invitation to the opening of "Different Spokes for Different Folks Bike Store". List the important information. Write the information on the invitation.

<u>Why</u> will the invitation be sent?
Store Opening
<u>Who</u> is giving the party?
Answers will vary.
<u>When</u> is the party?
_____
<u>Where</u> is the party?

Wheel On In!
Given by: _____
Time: _____
Date: _____
Place: _____

©1996 Kelley Wingate Publications   2   KW 1204

Worksheet 3

Name _____   Skill: Invitations

An invitation includes all the important facts.

"You are invited!" You must know <u>why</u>, <u>who</u>, <u>when</u>, and <u>where</u>. An invitation gives you all this information.

1. Read the invitation and answer the questions.

Come One, Come All!
Taft Park School
Talent Show

Given by: 4th Grade
Time: 7:00 p.m.
Date: October 20
Place: Taft Park Elementary School

<u>Why</u> has the invitation been sent?
School Talent Show
<u>Who</u> is giving the talent show?
4th grade
<u>When</u> will you go?
October 20 7:00 p.m.
<u>Where</u> will you go?
Taft Park Elementary

2. Write an invitation for a school open house. List the important information. Write the information on the invitation.

<u>Why</u> will the invitation be sent?
School Open House
<u>Who</u> is giving the open house?
Answers will vary.
<u>When</u> is the open house?
_____
<u>Where</u> is the open house?

ABC   OPEN HOUSE PLEASE COME!
Given by: _____
Time: _____
Date: _____
Place: _____

©1996 Kelley Wingate Publications   3   KW 1204

Worksheet 4

Name _____   Skill: Invitations

An invitation includes all the important facts.

"You are invited!" You must know <u>why</u>, <u>who</u>, <u>when</u>, and <u>where</u>. An invitation gives you all this information.

1. Read the invitation answer the questions.

RAE'S BOWL-A-RAMA
After School Special - Half Price Games

Given by: Rae Lowe
Time: 3:00 -5:00 p.m.
Date: Monday - Friday
Place: Rae's Bowl-a-Rama Jefferson Avenue

<u>Why</u> has the invitation been sent?
Bowling Special
<u>Who</u> is giving the party?
Rae Lowe
<u>When</u> will you go?
Mon.-Fri. 3:00-5:00pm
<u>Where</u> will you go?
Jefferson Avenue

2. Write an invitation to a swimming party. List the important information. Write the information on the invitation.

<u>Why</u> will the invitation be sent?
Answers will vary.
<u>Who</u> is giving the party?
_____
<u>When</u> is the party?
_____
<u>Where</u> is the party?

YOU ARE INVITED!
Given by: _____
Time: _____
Date: _____
Place: _____

©1996 Kelley Wingate Publications   4   KW 1204

Answer Key

Name _____ Skill: Invitations

| An invitation includes all the important facts. |

"You are invited!" You must know why, who, when, and where. An invitation gives you all this information.

1. Read the invitation and answer the questions

IT'S OUR ANNIVERSARY!

Given by: Norman and Grace Davis

Time: 8:00 p.m.

Date: July 12

Place: 41 Ashley Drive

Why has the invitation been sent?
Anniversary Party

Who is giving the party?
Norman and Grace Davis

When will you go?
July 12   8:00 p.m

Where will you go?
41 Ashley Drive

2. Write an invitation to a barbeque. List the important information. Write the information on the invitation.

Why will the invitation be sent?
Barbeque

Who is giving the barbeque?
Answers will vary.

When is the barbeque?

Where is the barbeque?

COME JOIN US!

Given by: _____

Time: _____

Date: _____

Place: _____

©1996 Kelley Wingate Publications   5   KW 1204

Name _____ Skill: Invitations

| An invitation includes all the important facts. |

"You are invited!" You must know why, who, when, and where. An invitation gives you all this information.

1. Make your own invitation and answer the questions

Given by: _____

Time: _____

Date: _____

Place: _____

Why has the invitation been sent?
Answers will vary.

Who is giving the party?

When will you go?

Where will you go?

2. Make your own invitation. List the important information. Write the information on the invitation.

Why will the invitation be sent?
Answers will vary.

Who is giving the party?

When is the party?

Where is the party?

Given by: _____

Time: _____

Date: _____

Place: _____

©1996 Kelley Wingate Publications   6   KW 1204

Name _____ Skill: Addressing Envelopes

It is important to address an envelope correctly. An envelope shows who is sending a letter and who is receiving a letter. Name, address, city, state, and zip code must be placed in the proper places.

The sender is : A
His house address is : B
His city, state, and zip code are : C

The receiver is : D
His house address is : E
His city, state, and zip code are : F

1. Study the completed envelope.

A → Mr. James Beach
B → 843 South Street
C → Charlotte, NC 49211

D → Mr. Kyle Duncan
E → 19 Reed Road
F → Dallas, TX 58397

2. Address the envelope below with the information given.

The sender is:
Miss Kelly Tulver
181 Crest Road
Canton, MS 70125

The receiver is:
Mrs. Dianne Baker
89 Barron Street
Albany, NY 25736

A → Miss Kelly Tulver
B → 181 Crest Road
C → Canton, MS 70125

D → Mrs. Dianne Baker
E → 89 Barron Street
F → Albany, NY 25736

©1996 Kelley Wingate Publications   7   KW 1204

Name _____ Skill: Addressing Envelopes

It is important to address an envelope correctly. An envelope shows who is sending a letter and who is receiving a letter. Name, address, city, state, and zip code must be placed in the proper places.

Address the envelopes below with the information given.

The sender is:
Mr. Donald First
69 Short Avenue
Culpepper, VA 88547

The receiver is:
Mrs. Tanya Elliot
316 Grove Place
Knoxville, TN 26791

Mr. Donald First
69 Short Avenue
Culpepper, VA 88547

Mrs. Tanya Elliot
316 Grove Place
Knoxville, TN 26791

The sender is:
Ms. Nancy Smith
74 Duncan Drive
Trenton, NJ 69275

The receiver is:
Miss Gail Russell
637 Lark Street
Portland, OR 57812

Ms. Nancy Smith
74 Duncan Dr.
Trenton, NJ 69275

Miss Gail Russell
637 Lark Street
Portland, OR 57812

©1996 Kelley Wingate Publications   8   KW 1204

Answer Key

Name _____   Skill: Addressing Envelopes

It is important to address an envelope correctly. An envelope shows who is sending a letter and who is receiving a letter. Name, address, city, state, and zip code must be placed in the proper places.

Address the envelopes below with the information given.

The sender is:
Dr. John Little
45 Meadow Place
Providence, RI 95672

The receiver is:
Ms. Janet Munch
75 Robin Blvd.
Denver, CO 74013

Dr. John Little
45 Meadow Place
Providence, RI 95672

Ms. Janet Munch
75 Robin Blvd.
Denver, CO 74013

The sender is:
Mrs. Lucy Kline
909 Pine Ave.
Seattle, WA 44307

The receiver is:
Miss Pat Bullard
4405 York Street
Lansing, MI 56233

Mrs. Lucy Kline
909 Pine Ave.
Seattle, WA 44307

Miss Pat Bullard
4405 York Street
Lansing, MI 56233

©1996 Kelley Wingate Publications   9   KW 1204

Name _____   Skill: Addressing Envelopes

It is important to address an envelope correctly. An envelope shows who is sending a letter and who is receiving a letter. Name, address, city, state, and zip code must be placed in the proper places.

Address the envelopes below with the information given.

The sender is:
Dr. Mary Howard
344 Richland Avenue
Fargo, ND 77409

The receiver is:
Mr. Bob Alden
378 Sunset Blvd.
Tripp, SD 89345

Dr. Mary Howard
344 Richland Ave.
Fargo, ND 77409

Mr. Bob Alden
378 Sunset Blvd.
Tripp, SD 89345

The sender is:
Mr Harry Webster
40 Lincoln Lane
Tyrone, NM 34068

The receiver is:
Mrs. Kerry Rogers
670 Maine Street
Fairfield, KY 45569

Mr. Harry Webster
40 Lincoln Lane
Tyrone, NM 34068

Mrs. Kerry Rogers
670 Maine St.
Fairfield, KY 45569

©1996 Kelley Wingate Publications   10   KW 1204

Name _____   Skill: Addressing Envelopes

It is important to address an envelope correctly. An envelope shows who is sending a letter and who is receiving a letter. Name, address, city, state, and zip code must be placed in the proper places.

Address the envelopes below with the information given.

The sender is:
Miss Rhonda Walter
660 Third Street
Chicago, IL 55098

The receiver is:
Mrs. Carla George
23 W. 42nd Street
Tampa, FL 21563

Miss Rhonda Walter
660 Third St.
Chicago, IL 55098

Mrs. Carla George
23 W. 42nd St.
Tampa, FL 21563

The sender is:
Mr. Fred Barrow
216 Dawson Drive
Ogden, UT 66065

The receiver is:
Ms. Jean Kesson
44123 Jasper Avenue
Concord, NH 55460

Mr. Fred Barrow
216 Dawson Drive
Ogden, UT 66065

Ms. Jean Kesson
44123 Jasper Avenue
Concord, NH 55460

©1996 Kelley Wingate Publications   11   KW 1204

Name _____   Skill: Addressing Envelopes

It is important to address an envelope correctly. An envelope shows who is sending a letter and who is receiving a letter. Name, address, city, state, and zip code must be placed in the proper places.

1. Address the envelope below to a friend.

Answers will vary.

2. Address the envelope below to a relative of yours.

Answers will vary.

©1996 Kelley Wingate Publications   12   KW 1204

Answer Key

Name _____   Skill: Friendly Letters

A friendly letter has 5 parts: date, greeting, body, closing, and signature.

1. Read the following letter.

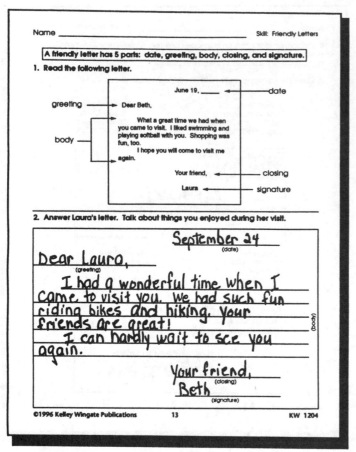

greeting → Dear Beth,

June 19, _____ ← date

body

What a great time we had when you came to visit. I liked swimming and playing softball with you. Shopping was fun, too.
I hope you will come to visit me again.

Your friend, ← closing

Laura ← signature

2. Answer Laura's letter. Talk about things you enjoyed during her visit.

September 24
(date)
Dear Laura,
(greeting)
I had a wonderful time when I came to visit you. We had such fun riding bikes and hiking. Your friends are great!
I can hardly wait to see you again.
(body)

Your friend,
(closing)
Beth
(signature)

©1996 Kelley Wingate Publications   13   KW 1204

Name _____   Skill: Friendly Letters

A friendly letter has 5 parts: date, greeting, body, closing, and signature.

1. Read the following letter.

August 6, _____

Dear Mike,

I had a good time riding bikes with you yesterday. The picnic lunch you packed was the best I have had in many years. Thank you for taking me along! Next week I will pick you up and we can go fishing in the mountains. See you then.

Love,

Grandpa

2. Write a letter to Grandpa. Talk about what you will bring on the fishing trip.

_____
(date)
(greeting)
Answers will vary.
(body)
_____
(closing)
_____
(signature)

©1996 Kelley Wingate Publications   14   KW 1204

Name _____   Skill: Friendly Letters

A friendly letter has 5 parts: date, greeting, body, closing, and signature.

1. Read the following letter.

September 5, _____

Dear Aaron,

School has started again and I think I will like 4th grade. My teacher is pretty nice and we do not have a lot of homework (most of the time). Best of all, we are going to study Egypt this year! Remember that Sphinx we made on the beach last summer? Now I will learn how they were really made!

Write soon,

Meyer

2. Write a letter to Aaron. Talk about things that are happening in your class.

_____
(date)
(greeting)
Answers will vary.
(body)
_____
(closing)
_____
(signature)

©1996 Kelley Wingate Publications   15   KW 1204

Name _____   Skill: Friendly Letters

A friendly letter has 5 parts: date, greeting, body, closing, and signature.

1. Write a letter to your Aunt. Thank her for the book she sent you. Include all 5 parts of a letter. Be sure to put a comma after the greeting and closing.

_____

Answers will vary.

_____

2. Write a letter to your Grandmother. Ask her to send you some of her special chocolate chip cookies. Include all 5 parts of a letter. Be sure to put a comma after the greeting and closing.

_____

Answers will vary.

_____

©1996 Kelley Wingate Publications   16   KW 1204

Answer Key

Name _____ Skill: Friendly Letters

A friendly letter has 5 parts: date, greeting, body, closing, and signature.

1. Write a letter to your Mayor. Tell him/her what is good about your city. Include all 5 parts of a letter. Be sure to put a comma after the greeting and closing.

Answers will vary.

2. Write a letter to your Mom or Dad. Tell they why you like being their child. Include all 5 parts of a letter. Be sure to put a comma after the greeting and closing.

Answers will vary.

©1996 Kelley Wingate Publications   17   KW 1204

Name _____ Skill: Friendly Letters

A friendly letter has 5 parts: date, greeting, body, closing, and signature.

1. Write a letter to your favorite TV star. Think of things you would like to ask. Include all 5 parts of a letter with commas after the greeting and closing.

Answers will vary.

2. Write a letter to your favorite author telling what you liked about his/her book. Include all 5 parts of a letter with commas after the greeting and closing.

Answers will vary.

©1996 Kelley Wingate Publications   18   KW 1204

Name _____ Skill: Friendly Letters

A friendly letter has 5 parts: date, greeting, body, closing, and signature.

Write a letter to one of your friends.

Describe yourself.

Answers will vary.

Tell what you like to do.

Describe your room.

Describe your family.

©1996 Kelley Wingate Publications   19   KW 1204

Name _____ Skill: Writing Paragraphs

A Paragraph contains a main idea and supporting details.

Every paragraph has one main idea. The main idea is called the **topic sentence**. It is usually the first sentence in the paragraph. The other sentences are details that tell more about the main idea. The last sentence retells the main idea.

1. Read the title, main idea, and details listed below.

Title of paragraph: My Teacher

Main Idea: Mrs. Black is the best math teacher I have ever had.

Details:
1. She explains math so I can understand.
2. She always answers my questions when I need help.
3. She gives just the right amount of homework.
4. She reviews the chapter before a test.

Retell Main Idea: Mrs. Black is my favorite teacher.

2. Use the information to write a paragraph. Include the main idea and details then retell the main idea. Indent the first sentence. Use capitals and periods. Remember to give the paragraph a title.

My Teacher

Mrs. Black is the best math teacher I have ever had. She explains math so I can understand it. She always answers my questions when I need help. She gives just the right amount of homework. She reviews the chapter before a test. Mrs. Black is my favorite teacher.

©1996 Kelley Wingate Publications   20   KW 1204

© 1996 Kelley Wingate Publications

CD-3719

Answer Key

Name _____   Skill: Writing Paragraphs

A Paragraph contains a main idea and supporting details.

Every paragraph has one main idea. The main idea is called the **topic sentence**. It is usually the first sentence in the paragraph. The other sentences are **details** that tell more about the main idea. The last sentence retells the main idea.

1. Read the title, main idea and details listed below.

Title of paragraph: Soup for Dinner

Main Idea: When mom lets me make dinner, I like to make soup.

Details: 1. I open the can carefully and pour the soup into a pot.
               2. I fill the can with water and add that to the pot.
               3. I stir it well while it is heating.
               4. I put the soup in bowls and add crackers.

Retell Main Idea: Soup makes a wonderful dinner!

2. Use the information to write a paragraph. Include the main idea and details then retell the main idea. Indent the first sentence. Use capitals and periods. Remember to give the paragraph a title.

Soup for Dinner
    When mom lets me make dinner, I like to make soup. I open the can carefully and pour the soup into the pot. I fill the can with water and add that to the pot. I stir it well while it is heating. I put the soup in bowls and add crackers. Soup makes a wonderful dinner!

Name _____   Skill: Writing Paragraphs

A Paragraph contains a main idea and supporting details.

Every paragraph has one main idea. The main idea is called the **topic sentence**. It is usually the first sentence in the paragraph. The other sentences are **details** that tell more about the main idea. The last sentence retells the main idea.

1. Read the title and main idea of the paragraph. Write your own details.

Title of paragraph: My Best Friend

Main Idea: My best friend is someone special.

Details: 1. Details will vary.
               2. _____
               3. _____
               4. _____

Retell Main Idea: I am glad I have such a great friend.

2. Use the information to write a paragraph. Include the main idea and details then retell the main idea. Indent the first sentence. Use capitals and periods. Remember to give the paragraph a title.

My Best Friend
Stories will vary.

Name _____   Skill: Writing Paragraphs

A Paragraph contains a main idea and supporting details.

Every paragraph has one main idea. The main idea is called the **topic sentence**. It is usually the first sentence in the paragraph. The other sentences are **details** that tell more about the main idea. The last sentence retells the main idea.

1. Read the title and main idea of the paragraph. Write your own details.

Title of paragraph: School

Main Idea: School helps me learn new things.

Details: 1. Details will vary.
               2. _____
               3. _____
               4. _____

Retell Main Idea: School is a good place to learn.

2. Use the information to write a paragraph. Include the main idea and details then retell the main idea. Indent the first sentence. Use capitals and periods. Remember to give the paragraph a title.

School
Stories will vary.

Name _____   Skill: Writing Paragraphs

A Paragraph contains a main idea and supporting details.

Every paragraph has one main idea. The main idea is called the **topic sentence**. It is usually the first sentence in the paragraph. The other sentences are **details** that tell more about the main idea. The last sentence retells the main idea.

1. Read the title and main idea of the paragraph. Write your own details.

Title of paragraph: My Favorite Holiday

Main Idea: My favorite holiday is _____

Details: 1. Details will vary.
               2. _____
               3. _____
               4. _____

Retell Main Idea: _____ will always be the best!

2. Use the information to write a paragraph. Include the main idea and details then retell the main idea. Indent the first sentence. Use capitals and periods. Remember to give the paragraph a title.

My Favorite Holiday
Stories will vary.

Answer Key

© 1996 Kelley Wingate Publications

CD-3719

Page 25

Name _____

Skill: Writing Paragraphs

A Paragraph contains a main idea and supporting details.

Every paragraph has one main idea. The main idea is called the **topic sentence**. It is usually the first sentence in the paragraph. The other sentences are **details** that tell more about the main idea. The last sentence retells the main idea.

1. Choose an idea for your paragraph. Write the title, main idea, and details. Retell the main idea at the end.

Title of paragraph: _Ideas will vary._

Main Idea: _____

Details:
1. _Details will vary._
2. _____
3. _____
4. _____

Retell Main Idea: _____

2. Use the information to write a paragraph. Include the main idea and details then retell the main idea. Indent the first sentence. Use capitals and periods. Remember to give the paragraph a title.

_____

Stories will vary.

©1996 Kelley Wingate Publications   25   KW 1204

Page 26

Name _____

Skill: Persuasive Paragraphs

A Paragraph contains a main idea and supporting details.

Some paragraphs are written to persuade, or change the way people think. These paragraphs have a main idea and supporting details.

1. You must convince your friend to let you borrow her new shirt. Ask her, give your reasons, then ask again.

Title :   The New Shirt

Main Idea: May I wear your new shirt to school?

Details:
1. It matches my pants so well.
2. It fits me just right.
3. The shirt is a good color on me.
4. I will hang it up in the closet when I get home.

Ask again: Please let me borrow your new shirt today.

2. Use the information to write a paragraph. Include the main idea and details then retell the main idea. Indent the first sentence. Use capitals and periods. Remember to give the paragraph a title.

The New Shirt

May I wear your new shirt to school? I matches my pants so well. I fits me just right. The shirt is a good color on me. I will hang it up in the closet when I get home. Please let me borrow your new shirt today.

©1996 Kelley Wingate Publications   26   KW 1204

Page 27

Name _____

Skill: Persuasive Paragraphs

A Paragraph contains a main idea and supporting details.

Some paragraphs are written to persuade, or change the way people think. These paragraphs have a main idea and supporting details.

1. You must convince your dad to let you have a pet bird. Ask him, give your reasons, then ask again.

Title :   The bird

Main Idea: May I have a bird for a pet?

Details:
1. I will keep it in a cage on the porch.
2. A bird is quiet and will never bark at night.
3. Cleaning the cage is easy so I will do it every day.
4. I am old enough to take good care of a pet.

Ask again: Wouldn't a bird make a great pet for me?

2. Use the information to write a paragraph. Include the main idea and details then retell the main idea. Indent the first sentence. Use capitals and periods. Remember to give the paragraph a title.

The Bird

May I have a bird for a pet? I will keep it in a cage on the porch. A bird is quiet and will never bark at night. Cleaning the cage is easy so I will do it every day. I am old enough to take good care of a pet. Wouldn't a bird make a great pet for me?

©1996 Kelley Wingate Publications   27   KW 1204

Page 28

Name _____

Skill: Persuasive Paragraphs

A Paragraph contains a main idea and supporting details.

Some paragraphs are written to persuade, or change the way people think. These paragraphs have a main idea and supporting details.

1. You must convince your dad to let you use his tools to fix your bike. Ask him, give your reasons, then ask again.

Title :   Dad's Tools

Main Idea: May I use your tools to fix my bike?

Details:
1. I will keep them in tool box next to my bike while I work.
2. The bike cannot be fixed without tools.
3. _Details will vary._
4. _____

Ask again: _Questions will vary._

2. Use the information to write a paragraph. Include the main idea and details then retell the main idea. Indent the first sentence. Use capitals and periods. Remember to give the paragraph a title.

Dad's Tools
Stories will vary.

©1996 Kelley Wingate Publications   28   KW 1204

Answer Key

Name _____ Skill: Persuasive Paragraphs

| A Paragraph contains a main idea and supporting details. |

Some paragraphs are written to persuade, or change the way people think. These paragraphs have a main idea and supporting details.

1. You must convince your brother to let you play his video game. Ask him, give your reasons, then ask again.

Title : _____Let's Play!_____

Main Idea: May I play your video game?

Details:
1. I will be very careful with it.
2. You can play the game with me.
3. Details will vary.
4. _____

Ask again: Questions will vary.

2. Use the information to write a paragraph. Include the main idea and details then retell the main idea. Indent the first sentence. Use capitals and periods. Remember to give the paragraph a title.

Let's Play!
Stories will vary.

©1996 Kelley Wingate Publications   29   KW 1204

Name _____ Skill: Persuasive Paragraphs

| A Paragraph contains a main idea and supporting details. |

Some paragraphs are written to persuade, or change the way people think. These paragraphs have a main idea and supporting details.

1. You must convince your mom to let you go bowling. Ask her, give your reasons, then ask again.

Title : Titles will vary.

Main Idea: May I Ideas will vary.

Details:
1. Details will vary.
2. _____
3. _____
4. _____

Ask again: _____

2. Use the information to write a paragraph. Include the main idea and details then retell the main idea. Indent the first sentence. Use capitals and periods. Remember to give the paragraph a title.

_____

Stories will vary.

©1996 Kelley Wingate Publications   30   KW 1204

Name _____ Skill: Persuasive Paragraphs

| A Paragraph contains a main idea and supporting details. |

Some paragraphs are written to persuade, or change the way people think. These paragraphs have a main idea and supporting details.

1. Ask your mother's permission for something. Give your reasons why you should be given permission, then ask again.

Title : Titles will vary.

Main Idea: May I Ideas will vary.

Details:
1. Details will vary.
2. _____
3. _____
4. _____

Ask again: Questions will vary.

2. Use the information to write a paragraph. Include the main idea and details then retell the main idea. Indent the first sentence. Use capitals and periods. Remember to give the paragraph a title.

_____

Stories will vary.

©1996 Kelley Wingate Publications   31   KW 1204

Name _____ Skill: Compare and Contrast

| Some things can be both alike and different. |

1. Complete the circles by comparing and contrasting a balloon and a baseball.

balloon   baseball

contrast	compare	contrast
1. pops easily	1. round	1. hard covering
2. stretchy	2. play with it	2. used in sports
3. light	3. bounce	3. solid

2. Write 2 paragraphs below. In the first paragraph tell how balloons and baseballs are alike. Tell how each is different in the second paragraph. Indent the first sentence. Title your story.

Balloons and Baseballs
   Put a balloon and a baseball side by side. Do you see how they are alike? Both of them are round. You can play games with both. A balloon and a baseball will fly through the air and bounce.
   A balloon will pop easily. When you blow it up, it stretches. Balloons can float away. Baseballs are strong and hard. They are all about the same size. When you toss a baseball into the air it falls to the ground.

©1996 Kelley Wingate Publications   32   KW 1204

Answer Key

(Top Left - Page 33)

Name _____ Skill: Compare and Contrast

Some things can be both alike and different.

1. Complete the circles by comparing and contrasting a school and an office.

school   office

contrast	compare	contrast
1. place to learn	1. has desks	1. place to work
2. has a principal	2. is a building	2. has a boss
3. has students	3. has people	3. has workers

(answers will vary)

2. Write 2 paragraphs below. In the first paragraph tell how a school and an office are alike. Tell how each is different in the second paragraph. Indent the first sentence. Title your story.

_____

Stories will vary.

©1996 Kelley Wingate Publications   33   KW 1204

(Top Right - Page 34)

Name _____ Skill: Compare and Contrast

Some things can be both alike and different.

1. Complete the circles by comparing and contrasting a newspaper and a book.

newspaper   book

contrast	compare	contrast
1. large pages	1. has stories	1. small pages
2. current events	2. we read them	2. cover
3. many stories	3. sold in stores	3. one story

(answers will vary)

2. Write 2 paragraphs below. In the first paragraph tell how newspapers and books are alike. Tell how each is different in the second paragraph. Indent the first sentence. Title your story.

_____

Stories will vary.

©1996 Kelley Wingate Publications   34   KW 1204

(Bottom Left - Page 35)

Name _____ Skill: Compare and Contrast

Some things can be both alike and different.

1. Complete the circles by comparing and contrasting skating to riding a bike.

skating   bike riding

contrast	compare	contrast
1. put skates on	1. move quickly	1. sit on a seat
2. has many wheels	2. sport	2. has 2 wheels
3. wear on feet	3. way to move	3. has pedals

(answers will vary)

2. Write 2 paragraphs below. In the first paragraph tell how skating and riding bikes are alike. Tell how each is different in the second paragraph. Indent the first sentence. Title your story.

_____

Stories will vary.

©1996 Kelley Wingate Publications   35   KW 1204

(Bottom Right - Page 36)

Name _____ Skill: Compare and Contrast

Some things can be both alike and different.

1. Complete the circles by comparing and contrasting yourself and a friend.

yourself   friend

contrast	compare	contrast
1.	1.	1.
2.	2.	2.
3.	3.	3.

(answers will vary)

2. Write 2 paragraphs below. In the first paragraph tell how you and your friend are alike. Tell how the two of you are different in the second paragraph. Indent the first sentence. Title your story.

_____

Stories will vary.

©1996 Kelley Wingate Publications   36   KW 1204

Answer Key

© 1996 Kelley Wingate Publications

116

CD-3719

Name _____   Skill: Compare and Contrast

Some things can be both alike and different.

1. Choose your own topic to compare and contrast.

_____   _____

different	alike	different
1. _____	1. _____	1. _____
2. _____	2. _____	2. _____
3. _____	3. _____	3. _____

(answers will vary)

2. Write 2 paragraphs below. In the first paragraph tell how these two things are alike. Tell how each is different in the second paragraph. Indent the first sentence. Title your story.

_____

Stories will vary.

©1996 Kelley Wingate Publications   37   KW 1204

Name _____   Skill: Descriptive Writing

Adjectives are words that describe which, how many, what color, and what an object looks or feels like. Adjectives make stories more colorful and interesting. They help you "see" a story in your imagination.

Here are 5 adjectives that describe each picture. Write a paragraph about each picture using these adjectives. Write a title for your paragraph.

1. crisp   2. juicy
3. red and green   4. tart
5. yummy

What a Snack!
Apples are my favorite snack. I love to bite into a crisp, juicy apple. I can't decide if I like red or green apples the best. Red or green, sweet or tart, all apples are yummy.

1. bright   2. yellow
3. hot   4. high
5. far

Paragraphs will vary.

©1996 Kelley Wingate Publications   38   KW 1204

Name _____   Skill: Descriptive Writing

Adjectives are words that describe which, how many, what color, and what an object looks or feels like. Adjectives make stories more colorful and interesting. They help you "see" a story in your imagination.

Here are 4 adjectives that describe each picture. Add an adjective of your own. Write a paragraph about each picture using these adjectives. Write a title for your paragraph.

1. frisky   2. floppy
3. wiggly   4. cuddly
5. soft
(answers will vary)

Paragraphs will vary.

1. white   2. far
3. fluffy   4. soft
5. _____

Paragraphs will vary.

©1996 Kelley Wingate Publications   39   KW 1204

Name _____   Skill: Descriptive Writing

Adjectives are words that describe which, how many, what color, and what an object looks or feels like. Adjectives make stories more colorful and interesting. They help you "see" a story in your imagination.

Here are 3 adjectives that describe each pictures. Add 2 adjectives of your own. Write a paragraph about each picture using these adjectives. Write a title for your paragraph.

1. sizzling   2. gooey
3. spicy   4. round
5. tasty
(answers will vary)

Paragraphs will vary.

1. cold   2. sweet
3. wet   4. _____
5. _____

Paragraphs will vary.

©1996 Kelley Wingate Publications   40   KW 1204

Answer Key

Name _____   Skill: Descriptive Writing

Adjectives are words that describe which, how many, what color, and what an object looks or feels like. Adjectives make stories more colorful and interesting. They help you "see" a story in your imagination.

Here are 2 adjectives that describe each picture. Add 3 adjectives of your own. Write a paragraph about each picture using these adjectives. Write a title for your paragraph.

1. interesting   2. colorful
3. fun   4. exciting
5. active
(answers will vary)

Paragraphs will vary.

1. round   2. black
3. _____   4. _____
5. _____

Paragraphs will vary.

©1996 Kelley Wingate Publications   41   KW 1204

Name _____   Skill: Descriptive Writing

Adjectives are words that describe which, how many, what color, and what an object looks or feels like. Adjectives make stories more colorful and interesting. They help you "see" a story in your imagination.

Draw or paste a picture in each box then write 5 adjectives that describe each picture. Write a paragraph about each picture using these adjectives. Give each story a title.

1. _____   2. _____
3. _____   4. _____
5. _____
(answers will vary)

Paragraphs will vary.

1. _____   2. _____
3. _____   4. _____
5. _____

Paragraphs will vary.

©1996 Kelley Wingate Publications   42   KW 1204

Name _____   Skill: Descriptive Writing

Adjectives are words that describe which, how many, what color, and what an object looks or feels like. Adjectives make stories more colorful and interesting. They help you "see" a story in your imagination.

1. Read this paragraph.
   It was a nice day. Without warning, a storm suddenly blew in over the lake. We were afraid our boat would sink.

Here are some adjectives that help describe the sentences:
   What kind of day it was: Bright, sunny, lovely, warm, spring
   How the storm came in: quickly, gusting, swirling, howling, thundering, booming
   What the storm looked like: dark, cloudy, windy, blackness, inky
   What the people looked like: pale, tense, worried, frightened

2. Make the paragraph more interesting. Use the adjectives above or create your own to "draw a picture with words" of what has happened in the paragraph. Give the story a title.

Paragraphs will vary.

©1996 Kelley Wingate Publications   43   KW 1204

Name _____   Skill: Descriptive Writing

Adjectives are words that describe which, how many, what color, and what an object looks or feels like. Adjectives make stories more colorful and interesting. They help you "see" a story in your imagination.

1. Read this paragraph.
   The old truck sat in the driveway. Dad and Sam were working on it. When the they finished, the truck would be as good as new.

Here are some adjectives that help describe the sentences:
   What the truck looked like: old, dented, faded green, rusty grey, dull, dented bumpers falling off
   How Dad and Sam were working: hard, difficult job, slowly, patiently
   How the truck would look in the end: shiny, glossy, bright, new

2. Make the paragraph more interesting. Use the adjectives above or create your own to "draw a picture with words" of what has happened in the paragraph. Give the story a title.

Paragraphs will vary.

©1996 Kelley Wingate Publications   44   KW 1204

Answer Key

Name _____ Skill: Descriptive Writing

Adjectives are words that describe which, how many, what color, and what an object looks or feels like. Adjectives make stories more colorful and interesting. They help you "see" a story in your imagination.

1. Read this paragraph.

The Christmas tree was nicely decorated. A star was on the top. There were lots of presents under the tree.

Here are some adjectives that help describe the sentences:
How the tree looked: beautiful, red and silver, twinkling, sparkling, colorful, prickly, golden, shining
How the presents looked: lovely, green and gold, bright bows, inviting

2. Make the paragraph more interesting. Use the adjectives above or create your own to "draw a picture with words" of what has happened in the paragraph. Give the story a title.

Paragraphs will vary.

©1996 Kelley Wingate Publications   45   KW 1204

Name _____ Skill: Descriptive Writing

Adjectives are words that describe which, how many, what color, and what an object looks or feels like. Adjectives make stories more colorful and interesting. They help you "see" a story in your imagination.

Read the sentence below. Write adjectives in the work box to add description to the sentence. Use the adjectives to write an interesting paragraph. Give the paragraph a title.

The house on the hill looked frightening.

What did the house look like? Answers will vary.

What made it frightening?

Paragraphs will vary.

©1996 Kelley Wingate Publications   46   KW 1204

Name _____ Skill: Descriptive Writing

Adjectives are words that describe which, how many, what color, and what an object looks or feels like. Adjectives make stories more colorful and interesting. They help you "see" a story in your imagination.

Read the sentence below. Write adjectives in the work box to add description to the sentence. Use the adjectives to write an interesting paragraph. Give the paragraph a title.

My room is really a mess.

What makes your room a mess? Answers will vary.

What words describe the mess?

Paragraphs will vary

©1996 Kelley Wingate Publications   47   KW 1204

Name _____ Skill: Constructing Stories

Stories have a beginning, a middle, and an end.

1. Make up your own story by answering the questions about the picture. Use adjectives for description. Write complete sentences.

1. Who or what is this story about? _____
Answers will vary.

2. Where does this story take place? _____

3. How does this story begin? _____

4. What will happen next? _____

5. How will the story end? _____

2. Write a story using your sentences. Be sure to use capitals and periods. Remember to indent the first line. Title your story.

Stories will vary.

©1996 Kelley Wingate Publications   48   KW 1204

Answer Key

Name _____

Skill: Constructing Stories

| Stories have a beginning, a middle, and an end. |

1. Make up your own story by answering the questions about the picture. Use adjectives for description. Write complete sentences.

1. Who or what is this story about? _____
Answers will vary.

2. Where does this story take place? _____

3. How does this story begin? _____

4. What will happen next? _____

5. How will the story end? _____

2. Write a story using your sentences. Be sure to use capitals and periods. Remember to indent the first line. Title your story.

Stories will vary.

©1996 Kelley Wingate Publications   49   KW 1204

Name _____

Skill: Constructing Stories

| Stories have a beginning, a middle, and an end. |

1. Make up your own story by answering the questions about the picture. Use adjectives for description. Write complete sentences.

1. Who or what is this story about? _____
Answers will vary.

2. Where does this story take place? _____

3. How does this story begin? _____

4. What will happen next? _____

5. How will the story end? _____

2. Write a story using your sentences. Be sure to use capitals and periods. Remember to indent the first line. Title your story.

Stories will vary.

©1996 Kelley Wingate Publications   50   KW 1204

Name _____

Skill: Constructing Stories

| Stories have a beginning, a middle, and an end. |

1. Make up your own story by answering the questions about the picture. Use adjectives for description. Write complete sentences.

1. Who or what is this story about? _____
Answers will vary.

2. Where does this story take place? _____

3. How does this story begin? _____

4. What will happen next? _____

5. How will the story end? _____

2. Write a story using your sentences. Be sure to use capitals and periods. Remember to indent the first line. Title your story.

Stories will vary.

©1996 Kelley Wingate Publications   51   KW 1204

Name _____

Skill: Constructing Stories

| Stories have a beginning, a middle, and an end. |

1. Make up your own story by answering the questions about the picture. Use adjectives for description. Write complete sentences.

1. Who or what is this story about? _____
Answers will vary.

2. Where does this story take place? _____

3. How does this story begin? _____

4. What will happen next? _____

5. How will the story end? _____

2. Write a story using your sentences. Be sure to use capitals and periods. Remember to indent the first line. Title your story.

Stories will vary.

©1996 Kelley Wingate Publications   52   KW 1204

Answer Key

Name _____   Skill: Word Box Stories

| Stories have a beginning, a middle, and an end. |

Write 3 more words about the picture in the word box. Use the words to write a story. Be sure to use adjectives, capitals, and periods. Title your story.

THINGS TO THINK ABOUT
Who is this story about? Where does this story take place? How does this story begin? What happens next? How will you make this story end?

Word Box

girl	tired
yawning	nap
sleepy	dream
pillow	wakes

Nap Time

This little girl is very sleepy. She is yawning and thinking about her pillow. She is so tired she can hardly hold her eyes open. It is time for her to take a nap. What will she dream about when she sleeps? When she wakes will she be full of energy and ready to play?

©1996 Kelley Wingate Publications   53   KW 1204

Name _____   Skill: Word Box Stories

| Stories have a beginning, a middle, and an end. |

Write 4 more words about the picture in the word box. Use the words to write a story. Be sure to use adjectives, capitals, and periods. Title your story.

THINGS TO THINK ABOUT
Who is this story about? Where does this story take place? How does this story begin? What happens next? How will you make this story end?

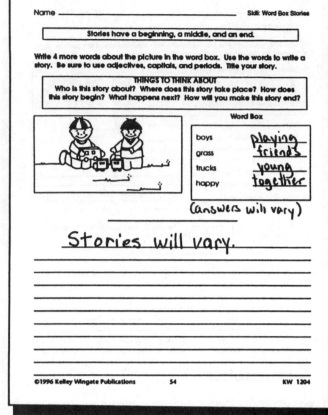

Word Box

boys	playing
grass	friends
trucks	young
happy	together

(answers will vary)

_____

Stories will vary.

©1996 Kelley Wingate Publications   54   KW 1204

Name _____   Skill: Word Box Stories

| Stories have a beginning, a middle, and an end. |

Write 5 more words about the picture in the word box. Use the words to write a story. Be sure to use adjectives, capitals, and periods. Title your story.

THINGS TO THINK ABOUT
Who is this story about? Where does this story take place? How does this story begin? What happens next? How will you make this story end?

Word Box

bed	soft
sleeping	pillow
blanket	warm
dream	lamp

(answers will vary)

_____

Stories will vary.

©1996 Kelley Wingate Publications   55   KW 1204

Name _____   Skill: Word Box Stories

| Stories have a beginning, a middle, and an end. |

Write 6 more words about the picture in the word box. Use the words to write a story. Be sure to use adjectives, capitals, and periods. Title your story.

THINGS TO THINK ABOUT
Who is this story about? Where does this story take place? How does this story begin? What happens next? How will you make this story end?

Word Box

ocean	star fish
fish	blue
seahorse	swim
shell	adventure

(answers will vary)

_____

Stories will vary.

©1996 Kelley Wingate Publications   56   KW 1204

© 1996 Kelley Wingate Publications   120   CD-3719

Answer Key

Name _____   Skill: Word Box Stories

| Stories have a beginning, a middle, and an end. |

Write 8 words about the picture in the word box. Use the words to write a story.
Be sure to use adjectives, capitals, and periods. Title your story.

THINGS TO THINK ABOUT
Who is this story about? Where does this story take place? How does
this story begin? What happens next? How will you make this story end?

Word Box

race	cars
flag	zoom
checkered	speedy
fast	winner

(answers will vary)

_____

Stories will vary.

©1996 Kelley Wingate Publications   57   KW 1204

Name _____   Skill: Story Web

| Stories have a beginning, a middle, and an end. |

Use the words in the web to write a story about the picture.
Be sure to use capitals and periods. Title your story.

THINGS TO THINK ABOUT
Who is this story about? Where does this story take place? How does
this story begin? What happens next? How will you make this story end?

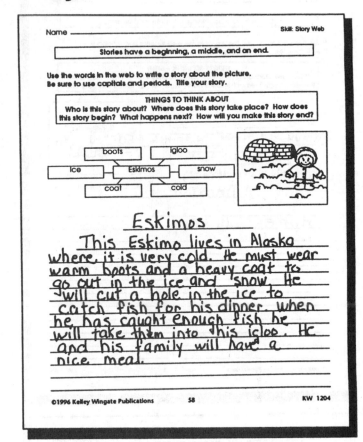

boots   igloo
ice   Eskimos   snow
coat   cold

Eskimos
This Eskimo lives in Alaska
where it is very cold. He must wear
warm boots and a heavy coat to
go out in the ice and snow. He
will cut a hole in the ice to
catch fish for his dinner. When
he has caught enough fish he
will take them into this igloo. He
and his family will have a
nice meal.

©1996 Kelley Wingate Publications   58   KW 1204

Name _____   Skill: Story Web

| Stories have a beginning, a middle, and an end. |

Finish the story web. Use the words in the web to write a story about
the picture. Be sure to use capitals and periods. Title your story.

THINGS TO THINK ABOUT
Who is this story about? Where does this story take place? How does
this story begin? What happens next? How will you make this story end?

feet   space ship
trolley   transportation   bicycle
airplane   motorcycle

(words will vary)

Transportation

Stories will vary.

©1996 Kelley Wingate Publications   59   KW 1204

Name _____   Skill: Story Web

| Stories have a beginning, a middle, and an end. |

Finish the story web. Use the words in the web to write a story about
the picture. Be sure to use capitals and periods. Title your story.

THINGS TO THINK ABOUT
Who is this story about? Where does this story take place? How does
this story begin? What happens next? How will you make this story end?

chicken   ants
sandwich   picnic   fun
basket   eat

(words will vary)

The Picnic

Stories will vary.

©1996 Kelley Wingate Publications   60   KW 1204

Answer Key

Name _____   Skill: Story Web

Stories have a beginning, a middle, and an end.

Finish the story web. Use the words in the web to write a story about the picture. Be sure to use capitals and periods. Title your story.

THINGS TO THINK ABOUT
Who is this story about? Where does this story take place? How does this story begin? What happens next? How will you make this story end?

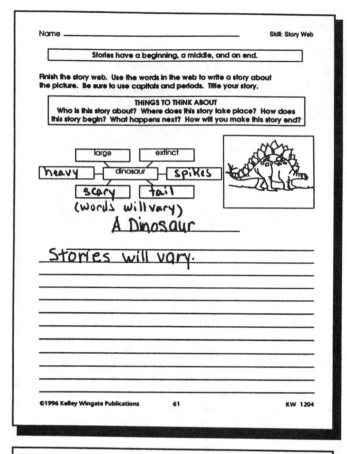

A Dinosaur

Stories will vary.

Name _____   Skill: Story Web

Stories have a beginning, a middle, and an end.

Choose a topic and fill in the story web. Use the words in the web to write a story. Be sure to use capitals and periods. Title your story.

THINGS TO THINK ABOUT
Who is this story about? Where does this story take place? How does this story begin? What happens next? How will you make this story end?

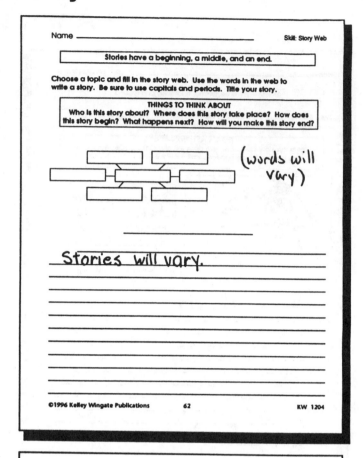

(words will vary)

Stories will vary.

Name _____   Skill: Writing Stories

THINGS TO THINK ABOUT FOR EVERY STORY:

★ Sentences begin with capitals and end with periods, question marks, or exclamation marks.
★ A paragraph contains a main idea and supporting details.
★ The first sentence of a paragraph should be indented.
★ Adjectives make stories more colorful and interesting.
★ A story tells who did what, when and where it was done, how it happened, and why it happened.
★ Stories have a beginning, a middle, and an end.

Write a story about the picture below. Be sure to follow all the hints in the "Things to Think About" box. Give your story a title.

Stories will vary.

Name _____   Skill: Writing Stories

THINGS TO THINK ABOUT FOR EVERY STORY:

★ Sentences begin with capitals and end with periods, question marks, or exclamation marks.
★ A paragraph contains a main idea and supporting details.
★ The first sentence of a paragraph should be indented.
★ Adjectives make stories more colorful and interesting.
★ A story tells who did what, when and where it was done, how it happened, and why it happened.
★ Stories have a beginning, a middle, and an end.

Write a story about the picture below. Be sure to follow all the hints in the "Things to Think About" box. Give your story a title.

Stories will vary.

Answer Key

Name _____   Skill: Writing Stories

THINGS TO THINK ABOUT FOR EVERY STORY:

★ Sentences begin with capitals and end with periods, question marks, or exclamation marks.
★ A paragraph contains a main idea and supporting details.
★ The first sentence of a paragraph should be indented.
★ Adjectives make stories more colorful and interesting.
★ A story tells who did what, when and where it was done, how it happened, and why it happened.
★ Stories have a beginning, a middle, and an end.

Write a story about the picture below. Be sure to follow all the hints in the "Things to Think About" box. Give your story a title.

Stories will vary.

©1996 Kelley Wingate Publications   65   KW 1204

Name _____   Skill: Writing Stories

THINGS TO THINK ABOUT FOR EVERY STORY:

★ Sentences begin with capitals and end with periods, question marks, or exclamation marks.
★ A paragraph contains a main idea and supporting details.
★ The first sentence of a paragraph should be indented.
★ Adjectives make stories more colorful and interesting.
★ A story tells who did what, when and where it was done, how it happened, and why it happened.
★ Stories have a beginning, a middle, and an end.

Write a story about the picture below. Be sure to follow all the hints in the "Things to Think About" box. Give your story a title.

Stories will vary.

©1996 Kelley Wingate Publications   66   KW 1204

Name _____   Skill: Writing Stories

THINGS TO THINK ABOUT FOR EVERY STORY:

★ Sentences begin with capitals and end with periods, question marks, or exclamation marks.
★ A paragraph contains a main idea and supporting details.
★ The first sentence of a paragraph should be indented.
★ Adjectives make stories more colorful and interesting.
★ A story tells who did what, when and where it was done, how it happened, and why it happened.
★ Stories have a beginning, a middle, and an end.

Write a story about the picture below. Be sure to follow all the hints in the "Things to Think About" box. Give your story a title.

Stories will vary.

©1996 Kelley Wingate Publications   67   KW 1204

Name _____   Skill: Three Paragraph Stories

Putting Paragraphs Together

★ An opening paragraph gives the topic of the story. It should catch the interest of the reader.
★ The second paragraph gives more information about the topic of the story.
★ The last paragraph reviews the main idea and ends the story.
★ Each paragraph contains a main idea and supporting details.

Use the information contained in this outline to write a three paragraph story. Use an additional sheet of paper if you need more space.

Title: My Pet
Main Idea: I.   New puppy
Details: A. Snaps at my heels
                     B. Named him Nip
                     C. Brown and White

Main Idea: II. Noisy and playful
                     A. Barks all night
                     B. Chewed up my shoes
                     C. Chases his tail

Main Idea: III. Love my puppy
                     A. Train him
                     B. Teach him tricks
                     C. We are best friends

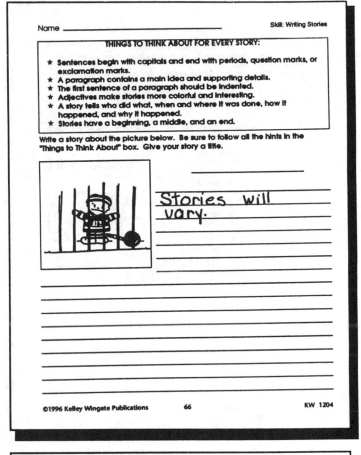

My Pet

I have a new puppy. He snaps at my heels. I named him Nip. He is brown and white.

Nip is noisy and playful. Sometimes he barks all night. Yesterday Nip chewed up my shoes. He loves to chase his tail.

I love my puppy. I will train him and teach him tricks. We are best friends.

©1996 Kelley Wingate Publications   68   KW 1204

Answer Key

Name _____   Skill: Three Paragraph Stories

Putting Paragraphs Together
★ An opening paragraph gives the topic of the story. It should catch the interest of the reader.
★ The second paragraph gives more information about the topic of the story.
★ The last paragraph reviews the main idea and ends the story.
★ Each paragraph contains a main idea and supporting details.

Complete the outline below. Use the information to write a three paragraph story. Add your own details. Use an additional sheet of paper if you need more space.

Title: The Terrible Storm
Main Idea: I. Storm began to rage
Details: A. Wind began to blow
                     B. Thunder and lightening
                     C. Rain

Main Idea: II. Power went out
                     A. House went dark
                     B. Candles for light
                     C. Spooky

Main Idea: III. Great time
                     A. Played hiding games
                     B. Told ghost stories
                     C. Scared each other

(details will vary)

The Terrible Storm
Stories will vary.

_____
_____
_____
_____
_____
_____
_____

©1996 Kelley Wingate Publications   69   KW 1204

Name _____   Skill: Three Paragraph Stories

Putting Paragraphs Together
★ An opening paragraph gives the topic of the story. It should catch the interest of the reader.
★ The second paragraph gives more information about the topic of the story.
★ The last paragraph reviews the main idea and ends the story.
★ Each paragraph contains a main idea and supporting details.

Complete the outline below. Use the information to write a three paragraph story. Add your own details. Use an additional sheet of paper if you need more space.

Title: The Accident
Main Idea: I. Broke my leg
Details: A. Riding my bike
                     B. Big tree in my path
                     C. Hit the tree

Main Idea: II. Went to the hospital
                     A. Mom took me in the car
                     B. Doctor took x-rays
                     C. Doctor set my leg

Main Idea: III. Home at last
                     A. Walking on crutches
                     B. Cast signed by friends
                     C. Feeling better

(details will vary)

The Accident
Stories will vary.

_____
_____
_____
_____
_____
_____
_____

©1996 Kelley Wingate Publications   70   KW 1204

Name _____   Skill: Three Paragraph Stories

Putting Paragraphs Together
★ An opening paragraph gives the topic of the story. It should catch the interest of the reader.
★ The second paragraph gives more information about the topic of the story.
★ The last paragraph reviews the main idea and ends the story.
★ Each paragraph contains a main idea and supporting details.

Complete the outline below. Use the information to write a three paragraph story. Add your own details. Use an additional sheet of paper if you need more space.

Title: Where Are You?
Main Idea: I. Lost my little sister
Details: A. Shopping at the clothing store
                     B. Looking at clothes
                     C. Sister missing

Main Idea: II. Looked Everywhere
                     A. Walked up and down every aisle
                     B. Called out name
                     C. Could not find her

Main Idea: III. Finally found her
                     A. Saw her legs under the coats on the rack
                     B. Made her come out
                     C. Hugged her

(details will vary)

Where Are You?
Stories will vary.

_____
_____
_____
_____
_____
_____
_____

©1996 Kelley Wingate Publications   71   KW 1204

Name _____   Skill: Three Paragraph Stories

Putting Paragraphs Together
★ An opening paragraph gives the topic of the story. It should catch the interest of the reader.
★ The second paragraph gives more information about the topic of the story.
★ The last paragraph reviews the main idea and ends the story.
★ Each paragraph contains a main idea and supporting details.

Choose a topic and complete the outline below. Use the information to write a three paragraph story. Add your own details. Use an additional sheet of paper if you need more space.

Title: _____
Main Idea: I. _____
Details: A. _____
                     B. _____
                     C. _____

Main Idea: II. _____
                     A. _____
                     B. _____
                     C. _____

Main Idea: III. _____
                     A. _____
                     B. _____
                     C. _____

(Title, idea, and details will vary)

_____
Stories will vary.

_____
_____
_____
_____
_____
_____
_____

©1996 Kelley Wingate Publications   72   KW 1204

Answer Key

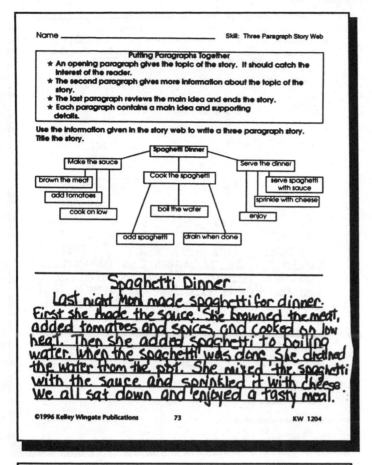

Putting Paragraphs Together
★ An opening paragraph gives the topic of the story. It should catch the interest of the reader.
★ The second paragraph gives more information about the topic of the story.
★ The last paragraph reviews the main idea and ends the story.
★ Each paragraph contains a main idea and supporting details.

Use the information given in the story web to write a three paragraph story. Title the story.

Spaghetti Dinner

Last night Mom made spaghetti for dinner. First she made the sauce. She browned the meat, added tomatoes and spices, and cooked on low heat. Then she added spaghetti to boiling water. When the spaghetti was done she drained the water from the pot. She mixed the spaghetti with the sauce and sprinkled it with cheese. We all sat down and enjoyed a tasty meal.

©1996 Kelley Wingate Publications   73   KW 1204

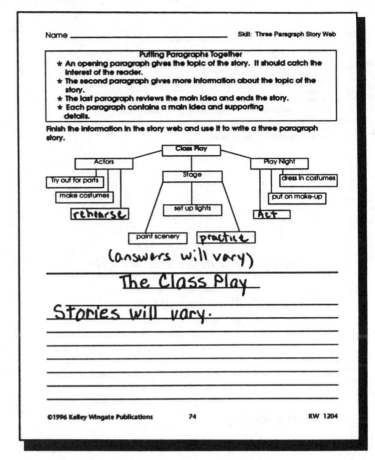

Putting Paragraphs Together
★ An opening paragraph gives the topic of the story. It should catch the interest of the reader.
★ The second paragraph gives more information about the topic of the story.
★ The last paragraph reviews the main idea and ends the story.
★ Each paragraph contains a main idea and supporting details.

Finish the information in the story web and use it to write a three paragraph story.

(answers will vary)

The Class Play

Stories will vary.

©1996 Kelley Wingate Publications   74   KW 1204

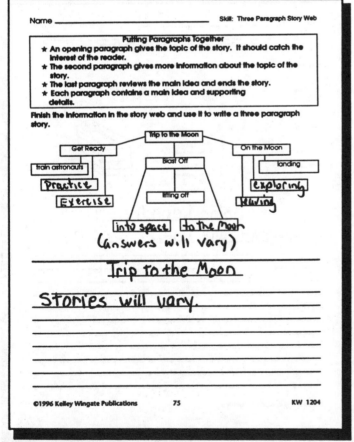

Putting Paragraphs Together
★ An opening paragraph gives the topic of the story. It should catch the interest of the reader.
★ The second paragraph gives more information about the topic of the story.
★ The last paragraph reviews the main idea and ends the story.
★ Each paragraph contains a main idea and supporting details.

Finish the information in the story web and use it to write a three paragraph story.

(answers will vary)

Trip to the Moon

Stories will vary.

©1996 Kelley Wingate Publications   75   KW 1204

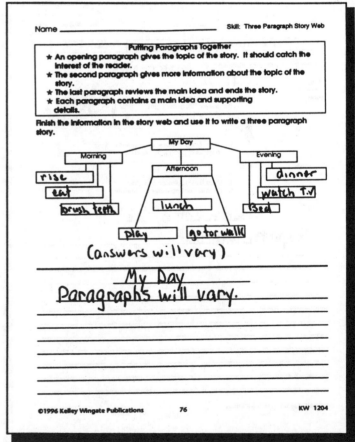

Putting Paragraphs Together
★ An opening paragraph gives the topic of the story. It should catch the interest of the reader.
★ The second paragraph gives more information about the topic of the story.
★ The last paragraph reviews the main idea and ends the story.
★ Each paragraph contains a main idea and supporting details.

Finish the information in the story web and use it to write a three paragraph story.

(answers will vary)

My Day

Paragraphs will vary.

©1996 Kelley Wingate Publications   76   KW 1204

Answer Key

© 1996 Kelley Wingate Publications

126

CD-3719

Name _____ Skill: Three Paragraph Story Web

Putting Paragraphs Together
★ An opening paragraph gives the topic of the story. It should catch the interest of the reader.
★ The second paragraph gives more information about the topic of the story.
★ The last paragraph reviews the main idea and ends the story.
★ Each paragraph contains a main idea and supporting details.

Choose a topic and complete the story web.
Use it to write a three paragraph story.

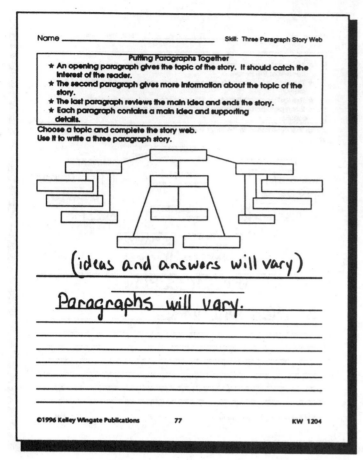

(ideas and answers will vary)

Paragraphs will vary.

Name _____ Skill: Writing Reports

A report gives facts in an orderly and clear manner.

Use the information contained in this outline to write a report.

Subject: Plants
Main Idea: I.   Importance to Earth
Details: A. gives off oxygen
                          B. homes for many animals
                          C. beautiful to look at

Main Idea: II. Parts
                          A. roots
                          B. stems
                          C. leaves

Main Idea: III. Needs
                          A. air
                          B. water
                          C. sunlight

Plants

Plants are important to the Earth. They produce the oxygen that we breathe. They provide homes for birds, bugs, squirrels and other animals. Plants make the Earth colorful and beautiful.
All plants, from flowers to trees, have roots, stems, and leaves.
In order to grow, all plants need air, water, and sunlight.

Name _____ Skill: Writing Reports

A report gives fact in an orderly and clear manner.

Use the information contained in this outline to write a report.

Subject: Bodies of Water
Main Idea: I.   Oceans
Details: A. salt water
                          B. covers 75% of the Earth
                          C. gives us food

Main Idea: II. Lakes
                          A. mainly fresh water
                          B. large body of water surrounded by land
                          C. gives us drinking water and power

Main Idea: III. Needs
                          A. fresh water
                          B. large flowing stream of water
                          C. gives us drinking water and power

Bodies of Water

Reports will vary.

Name _____ Skill: Writing Reports

An invitation includes all the important facts.

Use the information contained in this outline to write a report.

Subject: Doing Laundry
Main Idea: I.   Sort Clothes
Details: A. whites
                          B. light colors
                          C. dark colors

Main Idea: II. Wash
                          A. water temperature
                          B. detergent
                          C. load washer

Main Idea: III. Dry and Put Away
                          A. temperature
                          B. fold
                          C. put away

Doing Laundry

Reports will vary.

Answer Key

Worksheet (page 81):

Name _____   Skill: Writing Reports

An invitation includes all the important facts.

Use the information contained in this outline to write a report.

Subject: Writing a Report
Main Idea: I.   Before Writing
Details: A. brainstorm for ideas
                            B. look up information
                            C. make an outline

Main Idea: II.   Writing
                            A. get information and materials together
                            B. organize what you want to say
                            C. write a first draft

Main Idea: III.   Revise
                            A. read to check facts and organization
                            B. read to check spelling and punctuation
                            C. rewrite neatly

Reports will vary.

Worksheet (page 82):

Name _____   Skill: Writing Reports

An invitation includes all the important facts.

Choose a topic and put the information in this outline. Write the report.

Subject: _____
Main Idea: I.   _____   (Subject,
Details: A. _____   main ideas,
                            B. _____   and details
                            C. _____   will vary)

Main Idea: II.   _____
                            A. _____
                            B. _____
                            C. _____

Main Idea: III.   _____
                            A. _____
                            B. _____
                            C. _____

Reports will vary.

Worksheet (page 83):

Name _____   Skill: Point of View

The **first person point of view** tells a story as if the narrator were a part of it. This view uses the words "I", "me", or "we".
The **third person point of view** tells the story as if the narrator were watching it happen. This view uses the words "he", "she", "they", or "them".

This story is written from the first person point of view. Rewrite the story, changing it to the third person point of view. Add your own ending.

A Skating Disaster

I was skating on the sidewalk a few blocks from my house yesterday afternoon when a dog darted out of the bushes. The dog ran right across my path. Boom, down I fell! I stood up and brushed myself off. Suddenly a little girl ran out of the same bushes. The girl was calling, "Come back, Pixie!" As she rushed past me, I fell down again. I had just picked myself up again when a man raced out of the bushes! He was shouting, "Come back, Terry! Come back, Pixie!" I......

A Skating Disaster
She was skating on the sidewalk a few blocks from her house yesterday afternoon when a dog darted out of the bushes. The dog ran right across her path. Boom, down she fell. She stood up and brushed herself off. Suddenly a little girl ran out of the same bushes. The girl was calling, "Come back Pixie!" As she rushed passed her she fell down again. She had just picked herself up again......

Endings will vary.

Worksheet (page 84):

Name _____   Skill: Point of View

The **first person point of view** tells a story as if the narrator were a part of it. This view uses the words "I", "me", or "we".
The **third person point of view** tells the story as if the narrator were watching it happen. This view uses the words "he", "she", "they", or "them".

This story is written from the first person point of view. Rewrite the story, changing it to the third person point of view. Add your own ending.

Guess Who

Mysteries are my favorite type of book. When I start reading a mystery, I can't put the book down. I love to guess what will happen and try to solve the puzzle before I get to the ending. I get so caught up in the story that I forget all about time! Last night I began reading a mystery about a man who disappeared without a trace. It was such a good story that I didn't realize the time until the clock struck midnight. Suddenly.....

Guess Who

Endings will vary.

Answer Key

(Top Left)

Name _____   Skill: Point of View

The **first person point of view** tells a story as if the narrator were a part of it. This view uses the words "I", "me", or "we".
The **third person point of view** tells the story as if the narrator were watching it happen. This view uses the words "he", "she", "they", or "them".

This story is written from the first person point of view. Rewrite the story, changing it to the third person point of view. Add your own ending.

A Fire in the Oven

I am, without a doubt, the best chocolate chip cookie maker in the world. I measure just the right amount of flour, sugar, and salt. I mix these with butter, milk, and eggs. Then I add lots and lots of chocolate chips. Sometimes I take a little taste of the batter, and before I know it I have eaten half the cookie dough! Mmm, it is so good.

Last Saturday I had a little accident in the kitchen. I had just put the cookies in the oven to bake and the phone rang. I .....

A Fire in the Oven

Endings will vary.

©1996 Kelley Wingate Publications   85   KW 1204

(Top Right)

Name _____   Skill: Point of View

The **first person point of view** tells a story as if the narrator were a part of it. This view uses the words "I", "me", or "we".
The **third person point of view** tells the story as if the narrator were watching it happen. This view uses the words "he", "she", "they", or "them".

This story is written from the third person point of view. Rewrite the story, changing it to the first person point of view. Add your own ending.

Summer Camp

Last summer, Mark went to camp. He was gone for two weeks. He took his sleeping bag, flashlight, and bug spray. Mark camped in a cabin with three other boys. He made lots of new friends and learned many new things at camp. Every day he went swimming and he learned to paddle a canoe. Mark and his friends often went for hikes in the woods. Once they built a fire and cooked hotdogs and marshmellows over the flames. Mark.....

Summer Camp

Endings will vary.

©1996 Kelley Wingate Publications   86   KW 1204

(Bottom Left)

Name _____   Skill: Point of View

The **first person point of view** tells a story as if the narrator were a part of it. This view uses the words "I", "me", or "we".
The **third person point of view** tells the story as if the narrator were watching it happen. This view uses the words "he", "she", "they", or "them".

This story is written from the third person point of view. Rewrite the story, changing it to the first person point of view. Add your own ending.

Soccer Hero

Joey has been playing soccer for three years. His team is called the Mountain Lions. Joey plays goalie on the team. A goalie tries to keep the other team from scoring by standing in front of the net and blocking any balls kicked toward it. Joey is a great goalie. He played on the "All Star Team" last year. Last Thursday the Mountain Lions played a team called the Blazing Suns. The Suns were ahead by two goals. The game was almost over and it looked like the Lions were going to lose. Joey...

Soccer Hero

Endings will vary.

©1996 Kelley Wingate Publications   87   KW 1204

(Bottom Right)

Name _____   Skill: Punctuation and Capitals

Sentences and proper nouns begin with capital letters.
Sentences must have proper punctuation marks.

Place capitals and punctuation marks in the proper places. Add an ending to the story.

My Hollow Leg

My mom says I have a hollow leg. She says my stomach is not big enough to hold all of the food that I eat. All that food has to go somewhere. It must be going down into my hollow leg.

For breakfast this morning I ate six pancakes and five pieces of bacon. I was hungry long before noon. Mom and I went to Burger City for lunch. Mom had a small hamburger but I had the Burger Blast special (a triple burger, double fries, and a large shake). By 3:00 my stomach was growling again. I had to have something to eat. I had two peanut butter sandwiches and half an apple for a snack. I was really hungry by dinnertime.

Endings will vary.

©1996 Kelley Wingate Publications   88   KW 1204

Answer Key

Worksheet 1 (page 89)

Sentences and proper nouns begin with capital letters.
Sentences must have proper punctuation marks.

Place capitals and punctuation marks in the proper places. Add an ending to the story.

Creatures From Outer Space

Tim and I decided to camp out in the back yard. We got our sleeping bags, two flashlights, and some snacks. We unrolled our sleeping bags, laid down, and began to munch on some pretzels. It was a clear night and the stars were sparkling brightly. Tim found the Big Dipper and the North Star. One bright star seemed to be moving. We watched it race across the sky. Suddenly it stopped and began to grow bigger. It was coming toward us. It came to a stop right over our heads. Now we could see that it was not a star at all. It was a spaceship. A beam of light shot from the spaceship and glowed all around Tim.

Endings will vary.

Worksheet 2 (page 90)

Sentences and proper nouns begin with capital letters.
Sentences must have proper punctuation marks.

Place capitals and punctuation marks in the proper places. Add an ending to the story.

Lost In the Forest

It was a lovely October day. Beth and I took a walk in the woods to look at the red, gold, and orange leaves. We were not alone in the woods. Squirrels were busy gathering nuts for winter and deer were eating the last of the green grass. The sky was filled with flocks of birds flying south to warmer weather.

Just as we were turning to walk back, Beth spotted a small bear playing under some trees. We crept closer to get a better look. The baby bear saw us and cried out in fright. It began to run toward a large black rock. The black rock began to move and actually stood up. It was not a rock at all. It was the giant mother bear, and she was angry!

Endings will vary.

Worksheet 3 (page 91)

Sentences and proper nouns begin with capital letters.
Sentences must have proper punctuation marks.

Place capitals and punctuation marks in the proper places. Add an ending to the story.

My Fairy Godmother

Penny was not very happy. It was her turn to do the dishes again and she hated that job. Mother told Penny that after the dishes were finished her room needed to be cleaned. Penny grumbled to herself as she began to wash the dishes.

It seemed like all she ever did in that house was clean or wash something. She was beginning to feel a little like Cinderella. The only real difference was that she did not have a mean stepmother, and she had no sisters at all. Penny wished that she did have sisters. They could do all these dishes and clean her room for her. What a nice idea, but she knew it was impossible to have wishes like that come true.

A soft voice behind Penny called her name. Penny turned quickly and her mouth fell open in amazement.

Endings will vary.

Worksheet 4 (page 92)

Sentences and proper nouns begin with capital letters.
Sentences must have proper punctuation marks.

Place capitals and punctuation marks in the proper places. Add an ending to the story.

Watermelon Seeds

Mike's favorite food was watermelon. He ate it all summer long. He loved the sweet juicy taste. Mike never wasted a bite. He didn't even mind the seeds. He would just swallow them whole as he gobbled down each large, pink slice.

Uncle Roy often warned Mike about swallowing all those seeds. He told Mike that the seeds would sprout in his stomach and grow into watermelons. What would Mike do then? Mike would just laugh at the warnings.

The hot afternoon Mike ate three large slices of watermelon. He was about to have a fourth piece when he felt a strange rumbling in his stomach.

Endings will vary.

Answer Key

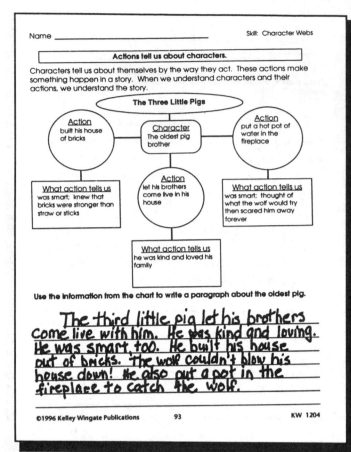

Name _____   Skill: Character Webs

Actions tell us about characters.

Characters tell us about themselves by the way they act. These actions make something happen in a story. When we understand characters and their actions, we understand the story.

The Three Little Pigs

Character: The oldest pig brother

Action: built his house of bricks

Action: put a hot pot of water in the fireplace

Action: let his brothers come live in his house

What action tells us: was smart; knew that bricks were stronger than straw or sticks

What action tells us: was smart; thought of what the wolf would try then scared him away forever

What action tells us: he was kind and loved his family

Use the information from the chart to write a paragraph about the oldest pig.

The third little pig let his brothers come live with him. He was kind and loving. He was smart, too. He built his house out of bricks. The wolf couldn't blow his house down! He also put a pot in the fireplace to catch the wolf.

©1996 Kelley Wingate Publications   93   KW 1204

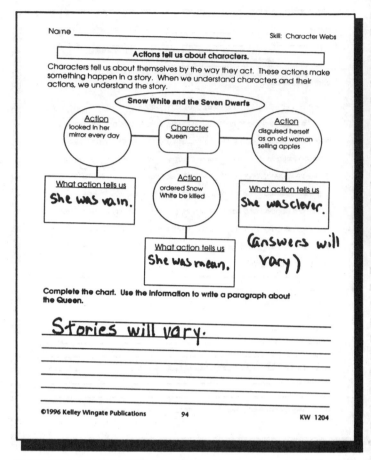

Name _____   Skill: Character Webs

Actions tell us about characters.

Characters tell us about themselves by the way they act. These actions make something happen in a story. When we understand characters and their actions, we understand the story.

Snow White and the Seven Dwarfs

Character: Queen

Action: looked in her mirror every day

Action: disguised herself as an old woman selling apples

Action: ordered Snow White be killed

What action tells us: She was vain.

What action tells us: She was clever. (answers will vary)

What action tells us: She was mean.

Complete the chart. Use the information to write a paragraph about the Queen.

Stories will vary.

©1996 Kelley Wingate Publications   94   KW 1204

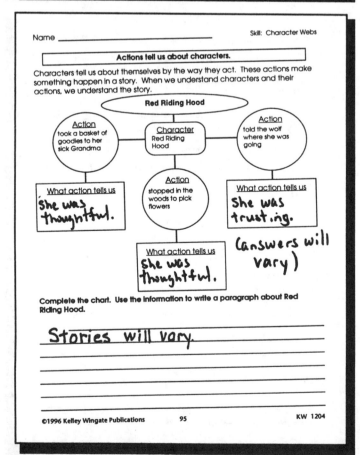

Name _____   Skill: Character Webs

Actions tell us about characters.

Characters tell us about themselves by the way they act. These actions make something happen in a story. When we understand characters and their actions, we understand the story.

Red Riding Hood

Character: Red Riding Hood

Action: took a basket of goodies to her sick Grandma

Action: told the wolf where she was going

Action: stopped in the woods to pick flowers

What action tells us: She was thoughtful.

What action tells us: She was trusting.

What action tells us: She was thoughtful. (answers will vary)

Complete the chart. Use the information to write a paragraph about Red Riding Hood.

Stories will vary.

©1996 Kelley Wingate Publications   95   KW 1204

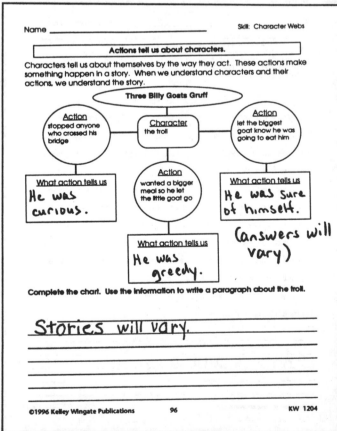

Name _____   Skill: Character Webs

Actions tell us about characters.

Characters tell us about themselves by the way they act. These actions make something happen in a story. When we understand characters and their actions, we understand the story.

Three Billy Goats Gruff

Character: the troll

Action: stopped anyone who crossed his bridge

Action: let the biggest goat know he was going to eat him

Action: wanted a bigger meal so he let the little goat go

What action tells us: He was curious.

What action tells us: He was sure of himself.

What action tells us: He was greedy. (answers will vary)

Complete the chart. Use the information to write a paragraph about the troll.

Stories will vary.

©1996 Kelley Wingate Publications   96   KW 1204

Answer Key

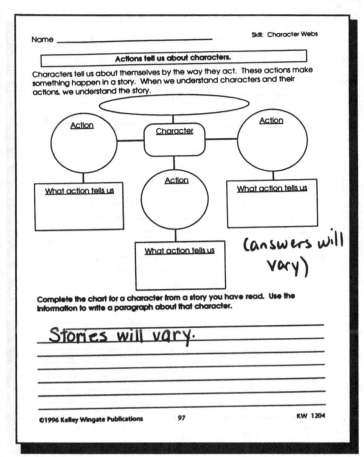

Name _____ Skill: Character Webs

Actions tell us about characters.

Characters tell us about themselves by the way they act. These actions make something happen in a story. When we understand characters and their actions, we understand the story.

(answers will vary)

Complete the chart for a character from a story you have read. Use the information to write a paragraph about that character.

Stories will vary.

©1996 Kelley Wingate Publications   97   KW 1204

Name _____ Skill: Book Reports - Story Elements

Book Report

1. Title: Reports will vary.

2. Author:

3. Name 2 characters in this book. Write a sentence about each one.
   1. _____
   2. _____

4. Tell where this story takes place. Write a sentence to describe the setting.

5. What is the problem in this story?

6. How is the problem solved?

©1996 Kelley Wingate Publications   98   KW 1204

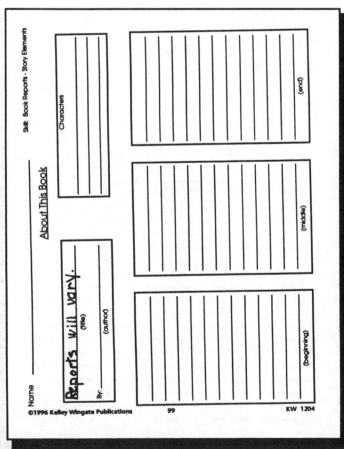

Skill: Book Reports - Story Elements

About This Book

Name

Reports will vary.

By: _____
(title)
(author)

Characters

(beginning)

(middle)

(end)

©1996 Kelley Wingate Publications   99   KW 1204

Name _____ Skill: Book Reports - Story Elements

Book Review

Title: Reports will vary.

Author: _____

1. Retell the story in your own words. Be sure to include the characters, setting, beginning, middle, and end.

2. Tell what you liked most about this story. Tell why and give examples from the book.

©1996 Kelley Wingate Publications   100   KW 1204

Answer Key

Name _____   Skill: Book Reports - Fiction Books

Book Report

Title: **Reports will vary.**

Author: _____

Where did this story take place? _____

1. Compare and contrast the main character with yourself.

     contrast   compare   compare

2. Tell what you liked or didn't like about the main character. Tell why and give examples from the book.

©1996 Kelley Wingate Publications   101   KW 1204

Name _____   Skill: Book Reports - Fiction Books

Reports will vary.
(Title)

_____
(Author)

_____
(Date Published)

My favorite scene from the book.

WHO ? _____

WHAT? _____

WHERE? _____

WHEN? _____

WHY? _____

©1996 Kelley Wingate Publications   102   KW 1204

Name _____   Skill: Book Reports - Nonfiction Books

Book Review

Title: **Reports will vary.**

Author: _____

Date published: _____

Subject of the book: _____

Review of the book: _____

Interesting facts learned from this book: _____

What I would like to know more about: _____

©1996 Kelley Wingate Publications   103   KW 1204

Name _____   Skill: Book Reports - Biography

Who's in the News?

Title: **Reports will vary.**

Author: _____

Date published: _____

Who this book is about: _____

Why is this person important? _____

What interesting things did this person do? _____

How did this person affect history? _____

How do you feel about this person? Why? _____

©1996 Kelley Wingate Publications   104   KW 1204

Great Job!

Receives this award for

_____

Keep up the great work!

_____

Signed

_____

Date

You Did It!

earns this award for

_____

Keep Up The Great Work!

_____
Signed

_____
Date

Congratulations!

Receives this award for

_____

Keep up the great work!

_____
Signed

_____
Date

Certificate of Completion

This certificate certifies that

_____

Has completed

_____

Signed _____

Date _____

Great Job!

Receives this award for

Keep up the great work!

Signed

Date

You Did It!

earns this award for

_____

Keep Up The Great Work!

Signed _____

Date _____

decorate	cuddly	crispy	crisp
dull	difficult	describe	dent
floppy	fade	envelope	dusty
glass	frisky	frightened	frame